# The Poison Widow

Linda S. Godfrey

PRAIRIE OAK PRESS
Black Earth, Wisconsin

Library of Congress Control Number: 2002114593

ISBN: 1-879483-88-2

Project Manager: Anne McKenna

Editor: Jerry Minnich

Copy Editor: Dawn Shoemaker

Designer: Colin Harrington

Printed in the United States of America by McNaughton & Gunn.

08 07 06 05 04 03 6 5 4 3 2 1

Prairie Oak Press, a division of Trails Media Group, Inc.
P.O. Box 317 • Black Earth, WI 53515
(800) 236-8088 • e-mail: books@wistrails.com
www.trailsbooks.com

# Table of Contents

# Acknowledgments

I am both grateful and indebted to all the following individuals, organizations, and publications for their generous assistance in researching and documenting the story of ***The Poison Widow:*** Kathlyn Gay and the other surviving members of the McGarrahan family, Adam F. Wooten, D.O., the Palmyra Historical Society, the Palmyra Public Library, the Walworth County Historical Society, the Wisconsin Historical Society Archives Department, the *Elkhorn Independent*, Frank Eames, Ed Messerschmidt, Clara Pierce, Doris Wise, Lena Yakes, the *Milwaukee Journal-Sentinel*, Fred Kraege, the Waupun Public Library, Whitewater's Irvin Young Memorial Library, the University of Wisconsin–Whitewater Library and Archives, the *Whitewater Register*, and my patient husband, Steven Godfrey.

*Linda S. Godfrey*
*September 2002*
*Elkhorn, Wisconsin*

# Foreword

"How much do you know about Myrtle McGarrahan?" Linda Godfrey asked the day she came to my mother's home in Zion, Illinois. The purpose of the visit was to interview my mother and me to gain information about Myrtle Schaude, who became the second wife of my grandfather Charles McGarrahan (deceased). I thought perhaps Linda was working on a genealogy. But instead she had a book in mind.

As an author of dozens of nonfiction books myself, I had to wonder what was so interesting about Myrtle. What had I missed? Was there an idea right under my nose that I had overlooked? What would inspire a book-length manuscript? "Well," said Linda, "You'd better sit down. This may be a shock." Indeed. Today, that seems an understatement.

The afternoon of Linda's visit, she told my mother and me about researching the trial of Myrtle Schaude in Wisconsin. Yes, she was the same Myrtle who had married my grandfather. As Linda went on with her story about how this woman poisoned her first husband and tried to kill her own children, I could only think: impossible, incredible! How could the person who became known as the "Poison Widow" be the same Grandma Mc we knew?

As bits and pieces of the story began to unfold, supported by newspaper accounts, I became certain this was a story that should be told in book form. My mother kept shaking her head. She refused to believe. "This couldn't be the same Myrtle [I] knew," Mom said. After all, Myrtle had been a housekeeper in my mother's home; she had cared for my mother's mother; she had cooked meals for the family; she had done exquisite needlework; she had been an active church member; she had been a "typical" grandmother.

Over the months that followed I learned more and more about Myrtle's early life through Linda's e-mail messages and copies of additional newspaper articles. I reminisced with my brothers and my children about Grandma Mc ... what did they think of her? Had they ever had a clue? I wished that I could have talked with my father's brothers, but all three of them were deceased. I did speak with an aunt, my dad's only sister, who was a teenager when her father, Charles McGarrahan, remarried. "Couldn't be the same Myrtle," she echoed my mother. But the facts speak for themselves. It not only could be but it was.

Now as this story is presented in print, I wonder, as do my family members, how could this person we knew as Grandma Mc keep her shocking past a secret over all the decades that we knew her? Of course, one answer is we didn't really know her.

Linda has provided a view of Myrtle that otherwise might have been buried forever in all the dusty court papers, newspaper accounts, letters, and other research materials. Readers no doubt will be left with a question that has been uppermost in my mind: how much do you *really* know about anyone?

Kathlyn Gay

*Florida author Kathlyn Gay has published many nonfiction titles over her distinguished career. Some of her most recent books include* Body Marks: Tattooing, Piercing & Scarification *(Millbrook Press),* Encyclopedia of Women's Health Issues *(Oryx Press),* Epilepsy: The Ultimate Teen Guide *(Scarecrow Press), and* Eating Disorders—Anorexia, Bulimia, and Binge Eating *(Enslow Publishers). Works soon to be released include* Abortion: Issues in Focus *(Enslow),* Encyclopedia of Death & Dying *(Greenhaven), and* Cultural Conflicts: The Ultimate Teen Guide *(Scarecrow).*

*Her Web site is www.ourworld.compuserve.com/homepages/Kathy.*

# Introduction

"He did it! He is a very bad man!"

Petite beauty Myrtle Schaude, sobbing as she took the witness stand in her own defense, hurled the accusation across the courtroom packed with shocked townspeople, relatives, and newspaper reporters. A small-town sex and murder scandal was just as sensational in "the Roaring Twenties" as it is now, especially one involving a respectable homemaker who confessed to poisoning her husband with strychnine and attempting to kill her four children, all for the sake of what one newspaper called "an unholy love."

The fact that it happened in the quiet, little town of Whitewater, Wisconsin, just blocks from a renowned teachers' college, helped make the courtroom saga irresistible to a nation just entering the age of mass entertainment. And Myrtle was either remorseful or clever enough to play her repentant widow part to the hilt, stylishly coifed and garbed, with just enough meekness to beg sympathy. She did blame her gawky paramour, Ernst Kufahl, as the instigator, but Kufahl eventually went free. His part in the case still remains very questionable, however, in this classic but complicated "he said, she said" case.

I came across the case accidentally while researching past Ku Klux Klan activities for a local newspaper. The year 1924 was an active one for Klansmen in the small towns around Walworth County, and it was while scanning that year's *Elkhorn Independent* on microfilm that I first spied "Poison Widow" headlines. I had never heard of Myrtle Schaude and couldn't find anyone else who had either. But I was hooked after the first article. That such a horrendous and once-famous case had been totally forgotten by the community was almost as intriguing to me as the story itself.

Besides the great melodrama of the story, there is also the timeless issue of motivation to ponder. At what point does a person who has led a relatively "normal" life, caring for others, bringing children into the world, and serving as a dedicated church member, cross to a place where her husband and children become mere impediments, removable at will? How does such a person decide that it's more important that she be able to pursue her romantic fantasy than that her family continue their lives?

According to *Crimes and Punishment: The Illustrated Crime Encyclopedia*, the psychological profile of a poisoner is that of an eternally immature person. A chapter titled "Poisoners" states, "Possibly the oddest thing about poisoners is that there is something in them that keeps them permanently immature, so they never grow up."

Perhaps, then, poisoners could be thought of as the "Peter Pans" of the criminal world. The same crime encyclopedia describes the 1876 death of an Englishman named Charles Bravo, whose wife, Florence, was tried for poisoning him with antimony. Bravo's pretty wife, who was not found guilty, nevertheless "had the temperament of a poisoner: the immaturity, the childish desire for her own way, the dreamy, romantic disposition."

At first glance it's hard to see this profile in Myrtle Schaude. Her attorney presented Myrtle as a model wife and mother, and indeed, she was believed to be exactly that by everyone who knew her before the trial. The Schaudes were faithful members of the local Methodist Church, where Edward was a trustee and sang in the choir and Myrtle was known for her charity in taking food to the sick. (She was never accused of hastening any deaths that way.) And her children were said to be "exceptionally fine" and well raised.

By all accounts, Myrtle was a very hard worker, even bringing home her own share of the family salt pork by serving meals to college students and keeping roomers to boot. If she had a fantasy life, she was adept at keeping it to herself. Who could possibly have known what the elegant housewife would prove capable of?

For someone who had never before deviated from the behavior society expected of her, it seemed Myrtle took to her forbidden liaison and the plotting of murders with sudden abandon. But court records show that Kufahl's influence played a big part in Myrtle's character transformation.

Was it possible she was just looking for adventure? With only an eighth-grade education, Myrtle had been married at seventeen to a man exactly twice her age. Compared to Ernst, the young ex-soldier, Edward may have seemed boring to Myrtle. Some speculated that he did not provide the affection she craved.

It could be that Myrtle told the truth in her testimony and that Ernst Kufahl was the one who prepared the fatal dose for her husband. Enough evidence was found against Kufahl to bring him to trial. But wherever the true guilt lay, they both would have gotten away with it entirely if Myrtle hadn't aroused the suspicions of the local coroner and district attorney by making a valiant and well-orchestrated effort to kill her four children, too.

The story may remind modern readers of Susan Smith, the South Carolina mom sent to prison for killing her two little boys by drowning them in the family car. Or the more recent case of Houston's Andrea Pia Yates who drowned her five young children, one by one, in the family bathtub. The husbands in those situations were much luckier than Edward Schaude, and Myrtle's child-murder plot was foiled in the nick of time. But if Myrtle had had her way, she would have wiped her whole family from the face of the fertile prairie earth.

It wasn't unheard of even in Myrtle's day, however, for women to attempt to kill their husbands and children, and some succeeded. One book loaded with such stories is *Bad Girls Do It* by Michael Newton, an encyclopedic listing including tales like that of Daisy De Melker. In South Africa in the 1920s, Daisy killed two husbands and five children with strychnine over a period of years. Annie Monohan, in the first decade of the twentieth century, poisoned three husbands and a niece in New Haven, Connecticut, with arsenic. In the mid-1800s in New Brunswick, New Jersey, Lydia Sherman earned the title of "Poison Queen" by dispatching three husbands, her own six children aged nine months to eighteen years, and two stepchildren. There are many more examples sprinkled through crime literature. Perhaps controlling what went into the gullets of those near and dear to them was one of the few real powers women of those times possessed, and some were not reluctant to abuse it for their own ends. It's amazing how many of them managed to avoid heavy punishment.

Myrtle Schaude had a knack for worming out of things like prison sentences, too, eventually managing to set up a whole new life for herself among an unsuspecting family who never knew of their stepmother's poisonous activities until long after she died.

This is the scary part. Myrtle Schaude lived and worked and made a place for herself in two communities, and in neither place did anyone suspect what was going on inside her or that she was capable of killing family members. One could argue that anyone who could do this is mentally ill, but it's very hard to diagnose a psychosis so long after the fact. (See the postscript by Dr. Adam F. Wooten.) But what makes Myrtle Schaude such a haunting figure is that a person so normal in every *visible* way could purposefully enact such tragedy. Many women have affairs, but few become murderous.

As the *Whitewater Register* said at the time, "Only in rare instances has the love for a man overcome the great inherent mother love for her children." A life like Myrtle Schaude's bears scrutiny from the rest of us, if only to pause and wonder … or shiver … at the sheer audacity of it.

The facts, quotations, and observations in this book have been drawn from a variety of state newspaper accounts; obituaries; more than 250 pages of court documents, statements, summaries, and testimony; records of pardon dockets and supporting papers; actual letters written between Myrtle Schaude and Ernst Kufahl (see Appendix); interviews with people still living who were present as young people at some of the incidents or who knew principals in the case; state prison records; and other local history documents and books.

The more I looked, the more I turned up. I am sure there are still more insights and aspects to this case that will be discovered only after the book is released to its readership. My main regret is that Myrtle's direct descendants (those I was able to contact) did not wish to contribute to the book and tell about the Myrtle they knew and loved.

Coincidentally, the district attorney who brought Myrtle to justice, Alfred Godfrey, was a distant relative of my husband. And Doris Duffin

Wise, who played with Myrtle's young daughter as a child and who nearly witnessed part of the tragedy firsthand, ended up as my next-door neighbor in Elkhorn many years later.

Although Myrtle's court testimony was biased, naturally, there seemed to be little question during the trial among those present that in most matters she was telling the truth. I leave it for the reader to judge just how truthful she was in the final analysis, and how much Ernst Kufahl really had to do with the death of Edward Schaude.

Here, then, is the amazing story of the woman who became known as "the Poison Widow."

# The Poison Widow

# Chapter One

## Unlikely Circumstances

*Whitewater, Wis. Dec. 10, 1922:*

*"Dear Ernst,* *Sunday Afternoon—*

*Dinner over and work all done went to church this morning and I read paper and some in a story book Ralph has from the library, and I guess this day will never pass . . . am wondering what you are doing this afternoon. Next Sunday afternoon we will be close by each other. . . .*

*"I wish you were here with me this afternoon. The children are out playing, or rather up to the Normal with Esther and Gifford Loomer on the swings, and the boys are over to Tafts and I am here all by my lonely. . . .*

*"I wish I was done with the Dentist. He told me I had one of the smallest mouths he ever worked in, it doesn't look so from the outside, does it. Ha ha. . . .*

*"Sakes alive I know you must be tired reading such a letter so will close and let you rest, guess I could write on forever. . . . Now I am going to slice potatoes for supper. . . .*

*"Sincerely, your little girlie. . . write to me tonight!"*

—excerpts from a letter written by Myrtle Schaude
to Ernst Kufahl

With her husband dead from strychnine poisoning the past ten months, and her lover Ernst Kufahl relocated from Whitewater to a lonely farm in McGrath, Minnesota, Myrtle Schaude dallied away a winter's Sunday afternoon sharing her innermost thoughts with Kufahl in royal blue ink on pink linen paper. At the age of thirty-seven, the dark-haired mother of four was considered pretty, even beautiful, by her friends and neighbors. She was endowed with the petite, slim body favored by 1920s fashion, and she always managed to look well groomed and stylish despite cooking daily meals for more than two dozen college students.

Nobody suspected yet that the pious widow, still a regular churchgoer and member of the Methodist Church, had anything to do with her husband's death. But friends and relatives may well have been wondering what was going on with Myrtle and her former boardinghouse roomer. If Myrtle's acquaintances had been able to read the daily correspondence between her and Ernst Kufahl, however, they would have known a lot was going on, and had been for some time.

And although Myrtle and Ernst could not have imagined it on that peaceful afternoon in 1922, in just less than a year Myrtle's letter plus a stash of other missives written to her by Kufahl, about three hundred in all, would be seized by the police, pored over for incriminating details, and read aloud in court as evidence against both of them. They would each be tried for the poisoning death of Edward Schaude, Myrtle's husband of seventeen years, and Myrtle would also be charged for the attempted murder of her four children by the same method. Myrtle did not take this turn of events quietly.

"Weeping and hysterical, confronted with the probability of a lifelong term in a state institution," read the *Elkhorn Independent* of September 27, 1923, "Mrs. Myrtle Schaude, of Whitewater, confessed slayer of her husband and instigator of a poison candy plot, in which she attempted to kill her four young children, nervously awaits in county jail the action of the court. While dozens of newspapermen, camera men and curiosity seekers, anxiously search for bizarre details of the tragedy in an endeavor to establish a motive for the crime, the District Attorney's office remains uncommunicative... ."

Myrtle remained hysterical in the jail for ten days after her initial confession, calming slightly only after finally making a second statement implicating Ernst Kufahl in the murder of her husband. Court records say she lay "squirming" on her bed, moaning, "Get that man, get that man! He is a bad man!"

According to the newspaper, she also constantly wailed, "Oh why did I do it, why did I do it," and the headline, "Whitewater Stunned at Story of Crime," indicated that her fellow townspeople were all asking the same question.

Strangely, this wasn't the first big strychnine poison murder case in Whitewater. About forty years earlier, wrote a reporter named Dewey Hamilton in the *Whitewater Register*, a poisoning crime of passion involved an employee of that newspaper office in the early 1880s. It was remembered by old-timers as "The Horan Case" and also involved three principal players: sisters Annie and Nellie Horan and a prominent shoe store owner named Fred Richardson who was Annie's fiancé.

Sister Nellie worked as a "compositor," or typesetter, in the *Register* office. Hamilton had been an apprentice at the time Nellie worked there, and he lived in a building with a room directly opposite the room Nellie and her sister shared in a building next door. He remembered hearing Annie's "cries, moans and groans" the night she died, although he didn't know what was going on at the time.

And what was going on, rumor had it, was that Annie was poisoned by Nellie because Nellie didn't want Annie to marry Richardson. Nellie fought her accusers, and although she was shown in court to have purchased strychnine for rat poison, she was acquitted and the crime was never solved. Her excuse was that she needed to kill rats at the *Whitewater Register* office, and the jury believed her. After all, she was a respectable woman. Nobody wanted to think a woman like that would do anything with strychnine but wipe out rodents.

Still, the Horan Case was forty years before Myrtle's time, and Whitewater, Wisconsin, had become a very different place in the thoroughly modern twenties. The repressive Victorian era was, if not entirely forgotten, at least out of recent memory. The First World War had been fought and won, Prohibition had changed the way the country imbibed, and Whitewater's growing State Normal School, or teachers' college (now the University of Wisconsin-Whitewater) was expanding so rapidly that the little town had to run to keep up.

Not that the town minded. The stately brick building known as "Old Main," which commanded a hill on the town's west side, was a source of both pride and income to Whitewater. The front page of each week's edition of the *Whitewater Register* was filled with student doings at "The Normal," and merchants multiplied on Main Street to supply the silk hose and woolen sweaters demanded by these fashionable young people. There were at least two pharmacies, several grocery stores, and a bustling assortment of places selling dry goods, hardware, and even newfangled automobiles. Myrtle and Edward Schaude owned a Ford sedan, themselves.

Whitewater had come a long way from its origins in the late 1830s when the first settlers discovered thirty abandoned bark wigwams near the shores of a creek with a sandy white bottom that the Potawatomie called "Whitewater." Pioneer Zerah Mead wrote, "The country was charming. The Indians had kept it burnt over every fall, so that when I came not a bush was to be seen. The old burr oak trees looked like orchards, the wild flowers were in gorgeous bloom, and the whole country looked like some gentleman's fancy park."

The city of Whitewater was laid out alongside two small lakes, Cravath and Trippe, which only added to the town's beauty. The larger Whitewater Lake lay a few miles southeast of the town.

The city could have remained a small settlers' outpost, but in 1852 the building of the Milwaukee and Mississippi Railroad depot made it a transportation hub, and by 1855 the little town had its first newspaper, the *Whitewater Gazette*. In 1857, Esterly Reaper and Mower Manufacturing opened and eventually made the town famous for its farming equipment, and in 1889 the world's only Spiritualist Temple, a college known as the Morris Pratt Institute and dedicated to the fostering and understanding of human psychic development, was built near downtown Whitewater.

While the Pratt Institute had nothing to do with what would happen to the Schaude family, it's absolute uniqueness lent an exotic air to this small Wisconsin town during the time Myrtle lived there. The Temple, according to an article in the *Whitewater Register*, October 18, 1918, was started by a trance medium from Madison, Mrs. Mary Hayes. Hayes said she received messages from a "controlling spirit" that claimed to be an old

German professor. While in a trance she supposedly received information about a rich bed of iron ore in Wisconsin and told her Whitewater relative Morris Pratt where to dig. When the mine paid off, Pratt built the temple. At least that's the story they told.

The newspaper ran regular notices of the Institute's well-attended Sunday evening programs, which boasted titles such as a 1924 offering, "Mediumship Explained." The building was famous for its third-story "white room," which was furnished completely sans color to better aid the meditation process. Most townspeople called the Institute either "Pratt's Folly" or "The Spook Temple." It closed its doors in 1932 and was torn down in 1961 to make room for a new telephone company building.

Openness to other forms of spirituality was just one example of the changing social climate in that era. As hemlines rose and women "bobbed" their hair, the old restrictions seemed to drop away with the long tresses. Small-town Wisconsin was still a conservative place; after all it was only little more than a decade since the showing of female ankles was considered amoral. But with all this new freedom of physical expression, people seemed hungry for more sensational tales of romance than had been allowed in public venues in the past.

The week of September 15, 1921, about the time Normal School students were settling in for the start of their fall semester, the movie playing at the Strand Theater in Whitewater was Allen Holubar's "Man-Woman-Marriage." Billed as "the love story of the ages," it promised nine unforgettable reels of barbaric beauties, pagan dancers, and "thousands of scenes that thrill and thrall." It was dedicated "for the women who struggle for Mother-Right … and the men who mock and deny that Mother-Right as men have since the world began!"

The following week's attraction listed in the *Whitewater Register* ad was a film called "Seven Years Bad Luck." It played, coincidentally, at about the same time Ernst Kufahl landed on the doorstep of the Myrtle and Edward Schaude home. There's no way to know if Myrtle saw the film, but the title proved unfortunately prophetic for her, and especially so for her husband, Edward.

# Chapter Two

## Little Spouse on the Prairie

Siloam, Wisconsin, was about as out of the way as a rural community could get in the late 1800s. North of the small village of Palmyra, plunked neither here nor there on the edges of Jefferson and Waukesha counties in the southeast portion of the state, Siloam was a tightly knit community of farmers who sat in one another's front parlors on Sunday afternoons and, come autumn, helped each other harvest the crops.

The neighbors were proud of their small, stone-covered schoolhouse and graceful Methodist Episcopal Church, the two hubs of social activity. Siloam was named after an ancient pool in the old city of Jerusalem, and the general area surrounding it was known as "Melendy's Prairie." The first homesteader, Daniel Melendy, staked his claim on the marshy flatland surrounded by burr oak savannas in 1837.

The occupants of one of these little farms, although originally from the town of Raymond in Racine County, were Henry Coad and his wife, Caroline Metcalf Coad. Caroline, known as Carrie to family and friends, married Henry October 29, 1882, at the age of twenty. Their marriage was soon blessed with a full complement of little farm workers: Jane (Jennie), Myrtle, Edna, Elizabeth (Libbie), and Frank.

Caroline Coad was a devout, lifelong member of the Siloam Church, according to her obituary, and undoubtedly saw to it that her five children were also faithful attendees. The four sisters and their brother probably also spent a large block of their time on farm chores, which would have been considerable in those days before modern machinery. The family was likely not well-to-do, and every member would have had to pitch in to make a living, but there is no indication that the Coads weren't reasonably happy or that they had a standard of living any lower than that of their neighbors.

Stone School, Waukesha County, Wisconsin, where Myrtle Schaude attended grades one through eight. *—Courtesy of Palmyra Historical Society*

The Coad children received their early education at the one-room schoolhouse built in 1845 on the intersection of County Highways Z and N. The school, described in *Historical Gleanings of Melendy's Prairie* by Clara Howell Pierce, was covered in stone ten years later by John B. Chapin, a stonemason whose children also attended Stone School. Boys and girls had separate entrances, each of which led into its own shelved coatroom where the children kept their dinner pails. The sexes were segregated within the classroom, too, with a tiny library corner on the girls' side. The boys

Promotions souvenir from Stone School, given to students at year's end, with names of Myrtle Coad and sisters. *—Courtesy of Palmyra Historical Society*

had to keep the wood box full if they wanted to stay warm, and water was hauled in by pail from the closest farm.

The school building was complete with classic bell cupola and two outhouses in back and was furnished with hardwood floors in 1884. It didn't get electricity until 1931.

The Coads' second daughter, Myrtle, went almost through eighth grade here. Why she never quite finished is not recorded—she merely stated in court later that she went *almost* through eighth grade—but her adult correspondence shows she was nonetheless able to read and write capably by the time she left Stone School. It might have been illness that prevented her graduation, or perhaps her family needed her to help out on the farm, a common cause of truancy back then. School records show she was there in 1901 at age fourteen, when the teacher was Ernest Uglow. Uglow was evidently a family friend, as later *Palmyra Enterprise* society columns mentioned Sunday afternoon visits to his house by Caroline and Henry.

Siloam Chapel, Siloam, Wisconsin. —*Linda Godfrey, 2002*

Myrtle's older sister, Jennie, married farmer Merritt Anderson, and the couple lived in nearby Union Grove. Myrtle stayed at home until she was seventeen. It was then that she caught the eye of a man seventeen years her senior, a newcomer who had recently bought a farm in the Siloam area and joined the Methodist Church.

The attractive bachelor was Edward Schaude (often spelled Schauda or Schade in older records), born on a farm just south of the little town of Rome in Jefferson County in 1871 to Phillip and Sophia Longenbach Schaude. The tiny village of Rome was described by one local historian in *Sullivan, Town 6 North* as "nestled in the picturesque intervale accompanying the swift-flowing Bark River."

Named for a town in New York State remembered by many of its early inhabitants, Rome may have been situated in a charming spot blessed with wooded hillsides, but it never obtained enough industry or transportation to attract a big population. Its chief claim to fame was being chosen as the site of the fictional 1990s TV drama "Picket Fences," which starred Tom Skerritt as a small-town sheriff.

Back in the 1880s and '90s, Jefferson County's rural base was suffering from a general decline in farming revenues that pushed many of its residents, especially young people, to big cities where they could find employment in industry. The county's population in 1890 was 33,530, more than a thousand fewer people than in 1875.

Edward Schaude must have been a scholar as well as a farmer, because he went on to graduate from the Normal School in Whitewater. He became a teacher, living at home until 1902, when he bought his own acreage a mile west of the Siloam church and adjoining the Coad property.

Edward seems also to have been a very religious man from his youth. His obituary in the *Whitewater Register* said he was raised in the German Evangelical Church in Rome, but upon moving to Siloam he transferred to the same church attended by the Coads. Because they were such close neighbors, he might have met Myrtle on an errand to her parents' farm, or it may have been at church. The pair was married two years later on Tuesday, October 4, 1904, at Myrtle's parents' home, as was the custom of the day.

The October 6 *Palmyra Enterprise* ran a front-page story about the wedding, and although the names were misspelled as "Shauda" and "Code," the paper called the bride and groom "estimable young people" with "a host of friends, whom the Enterprise joins, wishing them a long and prosperous life." The paper ran a fuller account of the wedding, with correct spellings, on the "neighborhood" page a week later.

The wedding sounded charming. Myrtle and Edward became man and wife at four in the afternoon, amid swaths of dahlias, asters, and evergreens. Myrtle's maid of honor was Myrtle Lean (probably a cousin), and Edward's best man was Delbert Burton. About forty friends and relatives were present for the ceremony conducted by Reverend C. I. Andrews, and the family provided a supper for their guests. After the meal, Myrtle and Edward were accompanied to the train station in Palmyra by the pastor and his wife. They were surprised there by a large group of well-wishers who merrily pelted the bride and groom with rice and old shoes.

Once safely aboard the train, Myrtle and Edward departed for a week's honeymoon in Algona, Iowa, at the home of one of Edward's sisters.

Their wedding photo was not published until years later in the *Palmyra Enterprise*, when the news about Myrtle's arrest broke. The photo is quintessential Victoriana; Myrtle's hair piled on her head in Gibson girl style, she wears a light-colored, shirred blouse with a high, pleated collar and what looks like a corsage at her neck. The pince-nez glasses on the bridge of her nose seem odd because none of the photos from her thirties show her in glasses (al-

Myrtle and Edward Schaude on their wedding day, October 1904.

though her prison medical records say she wore them for reading). The faintest hint of a smile plays around her comely lips. She probably was ecstatic to be marrying such a learned, propertied man, yet nervous to be leaving her parents for him. Of course her parents would still be right next door if she needed them, so it couldn't have been too terrifying.

Edward's face in the photo is inscrutable. His gaze is fixed directly into the camera lens; any expression of his mouth is obscured by the huge mustache drooping over his upper lip. His features are pleasant and even, however, and he is impeccably dressed in dark suit and starched shirt. He was probably happy to have found a young and attractive bride, even if she wasn't his equal in terms of education. But women of that day were not expected to be formally educated, anyway.

To all appearances, it looked like the proverbial match made in heaven. Little could Edward have suspected it was instead a match that would *get* him to heaven, quite before his natural time.

# Chapter Three

## Their Little Farm

*"On the hill among the pine trees,*
*Oaks and elms, and shrubs and flowers,*
*Stands the Minneiska Normal,*
*Where we've spent full many hours.*
*Called by us today Whitewater,*
*Known of old as Minneiska,*
*Love we both your names, dear Normal,*
*Our Whitewater,—Minneiska."*

—the 1921 Whitewater Normal School yearbook

Once Edward Schaude had moved his new bride onto his own homestead, they settled into farming and, as expected, started a family. Their first few years as newlyweds were marked by tragedy, however, when their firstborn child died as an infant. No cause was given in any of the available documents, and infant mortality rates being what they were in those days, the baby's death was not so unusual.

Ralph, the oldest son, was born in 1907, three years after the marriage. Delbert came along in 1910; the couple's only daughter, Mae, arrived in 1914, and the youngest child, Lawrence, in 1918. In 1912, between the births of Delbert and Mae, Myrtle had what she later called "a nervous breakdown" and was bedridden for weeks. "Nervous breakdown" was also the term used in her trial testimony, and no other description or diagnosis was mentioned or even attempted, leaving the true nature of her condition in some dispute. Her prison records noted that she did have scarlet fever at one time in her life but gave no date.

It isn't hard to imagine a young woman of twenty-five with two young children and all the other burdens of farm life having a tough time coping. "Nervous breakdown" was once a term applied to many little-understood disorders but now often looks a lot like clinical depression to us in hindsight. Because it occurred midway between births, postpartum depression was not likely, although it's possible Myrtle suffered a miscarriage at the time and wanted to keep it private. People were not open about "female problems" in those days.

Simple, physical exhaustion was also a real possibility. Myrtle testified later that she helped Edward in the fields when necessary, in addition to her household and child-rearing duties. And while she was a hard worker, she wasn't ever particularly muscular or physically robust.

Whatever the cause, Myrtle's illness as a young farm wife was of interest years later in her trial, because—coupled with her ten-day hysteria bout in the county jail—the possibility of a mental disorder could have been raised as a defense strategy.

Myrtle also never explained exactly why she and Edward decided to sell their Siloam farm and move to the outskirts of the comparatively bustling city of Whitewater. It may have been that neither the scholarly Edward nor the slight, stylish Myrtle felt cut out for fieldwork. It may also have been they were planning ahead for their own children to attend the Normal School more easily. Because it was Edward's alma mater, he certainly would have been well acquainted with the school and town. And being a former schoolteacher, he would have placed a high value on education for his children.

What we know is that in 1917 the couple sold their Siloam farm and bought thirty-four acres just northwest of the Normal School on land now occupied by apartment buildings, a student parking lot, and the University of Wisconsin–Whitewater's athletic facilities. More accurately, Edward Schaude did the selling and buying; Myrtle's name was never on any of the real estate documents.

They often referred to it as their "little farm," and the acreage was used mostly as pasture for the small dairy herd they kept so that Edward could have a milk business with a daily route in Whitewater. The farmhouse that came with the land was not as grand as many of the tall, gracious brick mansions that lined Whitewater's Main Street, but it had a parlor facing Pratt Street (now Starin Road), a kitchen, a spacious dining room that the family also used as a sitting room, and another room off the parlor that could be used for a master bedroom.

There were three bedrooms upstairs, and the family decided that with a little crowding, they could rent two of them to university students because the home was situated only about three and one-half blocks from the Normal School's "Old Main." The two older boys, Ralph and Delbert, were given their own bedroom upstairs, and Mae and Lawrence slept on a little pallet arranged at the foot of their parents' bed.

The master bedroom was not large by any standards, and its layout later became a matter of court record. The main bed was pushed sideways almost against the north wall, with a dresser to the right of it, close enough to the bed that Edward could keep a glass of juice or water within easy reach. With the children's bed adjoined, there was not much space left, but a "slop jar" was also a necessary furnishing because the house evidently did not have indoor plumbing other than a pump by the kitchen sink. In rural Wisconsin in 1917, this was life as usual and in no way reflected poorly on the Schaudes.

The Normal School had its own high school for teacher-training purposes, and oldest son Ralph attended there and was elected class secretary during his freshman year. The neighborhood was filled with college professors and their families, and the city's beautiful new library located on a parklike triangle of land near downtown was within walking or biking distance. The move must have been an exciting one for the whole Schaude family—even Edward, who soon turned his milk route into a thriving business venture. Myrtle testified in court that the family was both happy and prosperous while living there.

The Schaudes joined the large Methodist Episcopal Church and became active members. The church was highly regarded in the community, and the Schaudes were considered to have high standing within it. The *Milwaukee Journal* later reported that while Myrtle was not considered a "society" lady, nonetheless she associated with "the best people."

Whitewater was rich in church congregations of many denominations, but there were also many other sources of social interaction for most people. Between the Pratt Institute, the movie theater, and the worldly, educational influence of the Normal School with all its programs and events, Whitewater could boast a far more varied cultural environment than most small towns in Wisconsin. It was certainly more stimulating than living on a farm in the far boonies of the prairie.

The Schaude farm occupied an enviable location, just far enough outside the town proper to have a sizable acreage, yet close enough to be convenient and part of the Whitewater community. Would-be buyers made offers to Edward to purchase it from him now and then, but he had no intention of moving his family from their little Eden.

The house Myrtle and Edward lived in was occupied by others for many years after Edward's death, and then it was acquired by developers along with its parcel, which was named Harmony Hill Subdivision. The home was torn down in the early seventies to make room for multistoried student apartment buildings. A tiny photo taken by an assessor at the time shows it as a square, white, frame building. Because Myrtle had moved from it by the time she was arrested, newspaper photos published at the time of her trial showed only the house she purchased on her own after Edward's death, which is still in use by a campus fraternity. But Edward's house on his "little farm" remained private and safe from public scrutiny as long as it stood.

The only thing still recognizable from the Schaude farm is the little cemetery far back on the hill, on the northeast corner of the former Schaude property. And although none of the Schaudes was laid to rest there, it still seems strangely appropriate that the only thing remaining from the Schaude farm is a burial ground.

The Schaudes seem to have left few other imprints on the town. Myrtle's name was dropped from the church rolls soon after her trial. The current Methodist Church historian could find no photos of her with Ladies Aid Society members, and there are no Schaudes in the Whitewater phone book today. Myrtle Schaude seemed to be a person the people of Whitewater couldn't wait to forget. It's not surprising; such exploits as she confessed could hardly have been allowed to tarnish the reputation of the city or the Normal School. But of course if the Normal School hadn't been there, Myrtle would never have met Ernst Kufahl and might never have given the uses of strychnine a second thought.

# Chapter Four

## The Oddest Duck

*"You can call me Sweetheart if you like too* [sic]*. I know that you are mine. I will plan and surely expect to have you someday, and it can not be too soon. Good nite,*
*Sincerely yours, Ernst H."*

—excerpt from a letter written by Ernst Kufahl
to Myrtle Schaude, September 7, 1923

September was always an exciting month in Whitewater. The town's demographics changed as dramatically as the seasons when its rooming houses and dormitories swelled to bursting with new and returning college students. As evidenced by many classified ads in the local papers, it was common for families living within walking distance of the college to augment their incomes by taking in students and feeding them. Myrtle Schaude testified later in court that she always tried to keep two or three students in their farmhouse, handy as it was to the Normal School.

It must have been no great surprise, then, when a gaunt-faced young man from Watertown knocked at her door early that month in 1921, almost exactly two years before the letter that begins this chapter was written, and asked if he could rent a room.

At the age of twenty-eight, Ernst Kufahl was studying agriculture courtesy of the government in return for having served his time in the army during World War I. Kufahl had probably seen an ad the Whitewater Normal had placed in state newspapers that read, "The Business Courses Offer a Special Opportunity for EX-SERVICE MEN." The opportunity offered was a tuition break for veterans of the First World War, and many took advantage of it.

Kufahl, with his veteran status, was older than most students in his junior class were, and that may have been what set him apart from the others in Myrtle's quick eyes. She had one other male boarder that semester, Frank Brettschneider, who came a few days after Ernst Kufahl, but it was Kufahl who demanded and received her attentions. Brettschneider, said Myrtle in her trial, was "more studious," and kept to his own room. He was also a "government student," according to trial statements.

It's hard to say whether Kufahl's looks attracted Myrtle. That year's college yearbook, the *Minneiska*, put Kufahl's photo on page sixty-six of the Junior Class section. His dark hair combed neatly back off his high forehead, prominent eyes, and full lips faintly curved in slight smile gave Kufahl a pleasant enough appearance. Newspaper accounts at the time of his arrest also gave a positive impression of his looks, though the photo

Ernst Kufahl in the 1921 Minneiska yearbook of the Normal School at Whitewater, Wisconsin.—*Courtesy of the University of Wisconsin-Whitewater*

most of them published then—slack-jawed and bug-eyed in the glare of a camera flash—was not flattering. And Myrtle later described him as always looking sickly.

The caption at the bottom of the yearbook page reads, "The Juniors are the best of all, in their own estimation; We hope to see them back next fall in the Senior class, their destination." (At the time, the designation "juniors" seemed to cover all underclassmen.)

The wish to see the students back next fall might have been fulfilled for the other juniors on that page, but it wouldn't be for Kufahl, who began setting his own fate in motion within weeks of his arrival in Whitewater. The ex-soldier, it seemed, adapted to his new surroundings very quickly, and he soon decided what he wished his future to be.

According to Myrtle's court testimony, it was Kufahl who started their relationship by finding excuses to be alone with Myrtle in the kitchen. After a week or two of boarding with the Schaudes, Myrtle said, Kufahl asked one night if her husband would care if he helped her wipe the dishes. "I says, you better ask him," Myrtle testified. Kufahl did ask, and Edward didn't object.

Kufahl kept on helping Myrtle with the dishes, and he gradually took on the additional tasks of sweeping, dusting, setting the table, ironing, and even washing floors and mending the family's stockings. This is how Myrtle described it in her questioning at trial:

> *Q: He has often helped you carry food to the table from the kitchen?*
>
> *A: Yes, most every noon he would, and most every supper time.*
>
> *Q: Cut the bread?*
>
> *A: Sometimes.*
>
> *Q: Frosted cakes?*
>
> *A: He has some, yes. . . .*
>
> *Q: Quite frequently he was around the kitchen there with an apron on. Is that true?*
>
> *A. Very often.*

One could wonder if Edward Schaude might not have thought it strange that a grown man, an agricultural student and army veteran, would be so eager to perform what was then disdained as strictly women's work. Edward's eyebrows had to have shot up, too, when Kufahl took to wearing one of Myrtle's aprons while he did his chores. At his trial, the prosecution mockingly characterized Kufahl as "making a general hired girl of himself." But then, husband Edward certainly wasn't in the kitchen offering to help Myrtle. Perhaps Edward was even somewhat grateful to have free kitchen assistance from his roomer.

After about two months in the Schaude home, Kufahl returned from school one day and informed Myrtle and Edward that he had "been examined by an ex-serviceman, and the man told him he should drink more milk and eggnog," according to Myrtle. Kufahl needed three or four quarts of milk a day, specified the mysterious serviceman. So every day, the Schaudes made sure that Kufahl received eight to twelve glasses of milk, two glasses of eggnog, and two wineglasses full of thick cream.

Kufahl's illness may have been explained by the *Milwaukee Journal* when, in covering Kufahl's trial years later, it referred to him as "tubercular," even describing his "tuberculosis-pinched shoulders." The paper also said Kufahl had problems with his "organs" from contracting influenza in the service. However, the supposed tuberculosis never seemed to prevent Kufahl from attending his classes, helping Myrtle, or playing with the Schaude children on the farmhouse lawn, a sight the neighbors often observed.

It helped that Edward and Myrtle happened to have an abundance of dairy products, because they kept a dozen or so cows and Edward had his own milk delivery business. And Edward was adamant that Kufahl should have his nourishment. In the postwar years, people were still feeling very grateful to ex-soldiers, and there was a general surplus of dairy products across the whole country once war usage ended. Edward often asked Myrtle whether Kufahl was getting the milk he needed and admonished her to be sure to provide it.

Ever the obedient wife, Myrtle took on her assignment with zeal. If Kufahl couldn't drink enough milk at the meal table, either she or the children would take his servings up to his room. Sometimes, said Myrtle, she would send "little Mae" but more often ended up delivering the goods herself. The local papers later made much of Myrtle's testimony that she sometimes waited on Kufahl while "scantily clad," perhaps in a light dressing robe with not much on underneath, but these lightly dressed deliveries were actually made after Edward's death, if her testimony can be believed.

Still, improprieties soon began happening. Myrtle claimed that for a long time she simply brought the eggnog into Kufahl's room, set it on the table, and walked out. Eventually, she said, Kufahl began grabbing her arm and pulling her down on the bed beside him when she tried to leave the room. Myrtle insisted they would just sit there and "pass the time of day" at first, but eventually things changed as the pair grew more intimate.

The intimacies didn't all happen in Kufahl's room, either. For some reason, Myrtle and Kufahl at one time found themselves alone in the parlor, or "best" downstairs room. Neighbors at the time remember the Schaude home as being furnished simply but nicely, and the family was evidently well off enough to own an "Edison" turntable and a collection of records.

"I was putting a record on the Edison," Myrtle said, "and he grabbed hold of me and pulled me down in his lap. I jumped up quickly, and I says, 'What is the matter with you?' He says, 'I didn't do anything.' I said, 'I consider it something.'"

Another time, while Kufahl was bringing in water from the outside pump, Myrtle said he tricked her into placing her face against the window pane by telling her to look down at something outside, and then he kissed her from the other side of the glass. Then, he told her solemnly, she could never say that he "didn't kiss her through the window."

Kufahl didn't seem to care about the surroundings when he felt like making an amorous advance. Myrtle told how she was in the barn helping with the milking when Kufahl sat on a stool next to her, put his arm around her waist, and began rubbing her leg. She claimed to have told him to stop and do some milking himself, but he objected that he couldn't because he wasn't wearing overalls, probably still being dressed in the suit he wore to classes that day. This was risky behavior, because any of the family or neighbors could have popped into the barn.

By second semester, which started around the beginning of February 1922, Kufahl had arranged his classes so that he could be home with Myrtle during the day, between 10:00 and noon, while Edward was out and busy with his milk business and barn chores. Kufahl told fellow roomer Frank Brettschneider that he had fallen in love with Mrs. Schaude at first sight and that the two of them had exchanged letters with "endearing expressions" over Christmas vacation, while he was back with his family in Watertown. He enclosed one such letter with a basket of candy he sent the family as a present. But the letter bore a strange note at the top that read, "Iron me out."

"Probably just more of his nonsense," sniffed Edward Schaude when Myrtle opened the package in the presence of her excited family. Perhaps Edward was giving a clue as to what he really did think of his apron-wearing, eggnog-swilling boarder. He advised Myrtle not to waste good electricity but wait until the next time she did ironing and then see what it said. Myrtle took her very next opportunity to do so.

"Dear Ma," began the note oddly, "I am writing this with milk." (Kufahl often addressed Myrtle as "Ma" while he lived at the Schaude home, saying it was his way of teasing her because she didn't like her children to call her that.) After discussing his vacation at some length, Kufahl finished his note by saying he liked his home in Whitewater because there was "some little body there he was longing to see," adding he wished when he got back he could take her in his arms and call her "his." Needless to say, Myrtle never showed the letter to Edward. She claimed in the trial that she didn't think he would care about it, or she would have. But she kept the basket to use for her sewing.

As "Ma" Schaude and Ernst Kufahl grew closer and bolder in their affections, people began noticing that something had changed in the atmosphere at the Schaude house. A "scrubwoman" named Gertrude Wagner testified at the trial that she became aware of the new relationship on her regular cleaning visits, and she told the court she was sure Mr. Schaude had "lost his wife's love" well before he died.

If Edward had lost Myrtle's love, Ernst Kufahl had found it, and he wasn't giving it back. But he may have had his eyes on more than Myrtle's well-turned figure.

Kufahl began making pointed comments that Myrtle recalled in her testimony. He wanted to know if they owned their farm free and clear, and how much it was worth. Myrtle said they owed about three thousand dollars because of a mortgage on a small place they had "out west" (possibly Edward's brother's former farm in Buffalo County, Nebraska), but she wouldn't tell him the value of the Whitewater farm. Kufahl then went so far as to go to the house of a neighbor, Mrs. Taft, and call Myrtle from there, telling Mrs. Taft he wanted to "joke with Myrtle" and then pretending to be an interested buyer. He asked Myrtle if the farm was for sale, and she answered it wasn't. Kufahl then asked whether they would sell it if they got a good price. Myrtle, somehow not recognizing her boarder's voice, said she hardly thought so because they had been offered $11,500 and could have gotten $12,000. Kufahl, she said, began to laugh.

It seemed as if he were taunting Myrtle by making a point of phoning her and tricking her out of the information. After all, he could have made discreet inquiries on his own and never let her know about it. Perhaps he was trying to impress her with his power over her, his ability to get information whether she allowed him or not. At any rate, it was a very unseemly cat-and-mouse game for a boarder to play with his landlady.

Kufahl next began to take a keen interest in Edward Schaude's health. Around the beginning of March 1922, a month after Kufahl's return to the Schaude household, Edward was having what the doctor called liver problems, or "yellow jaundice," eventually suffering particularly from fatigue and loss of appetite. He started to vomit often and asked Myrtle for prune juice or eggnog to help soothe his "indigestion."

Myrtle noted that on one occasion before her husband took to his sickbed, Kufahl told her that her husband was sitting in the barn, not looking well, and that he supposed "the boss" would "croak" before long. Kufahl almost seemed to be gloating. "Oh, Ernst, how you do talk!" Myrtle said she replied. Kufahl then asked her what she would do if Edward

Myrtle Schaude, "The Poison Widow."

"did croak," and Myrtle told him, "If anything should happen to Ed my life would not be worth living anymore." Kufahl admonished her she shouldn't feel that way because she would have enough to live on, as if that were all she should be concerned with.

Another time, Kufahl asked Myrtle how old Edward was. She told him Edward was fifty-one. "Well the Mister is getting pretty old," Kufahl replied, "and he may die pretty soon, and I am going to wait for you."

The combination of interest in the family assets along with predictions of Edward's failing health seem damning, if Myrtle was accurate. And unfortunately, most of the testimony preserved from both Kufahl's and Myrtle's trials is Myrtle's alone. Whether Kufahl was not questioned as extensively is hard to say now—all there is to go on are the newspaper reports that he later denied any involvement in Edward's death—so it is Myrtle's word that has to be taken for most of the conversations. However, prosecutor and defending attorneys, as well as attending newspaper reporters, seemed to agree that Myrtle was for the most part truthful when testifying.

At Kufahl's trial, District Attorney Alfred Godfrey made sure the jury realized that Kufahl had access to the strychnine used to kill rats that Myrtle kept in an upper kitchen cupboard, and that Kufahl often helped make and serve drinks and food to the family at dinner. Was Kufahl lacing Edward's beverages over time, without Myrtle's knowledge, thereby causing "the Mister" to gradually become ill? It's possible.

It's also possible that Myrtle was looking toward having a younger husband and that the two were acting together or that Myrtle was spiking

Edward's eggnog on her own and just wouldn't admit it. A report in the September 25, 1923, *Milwaukee Journal* claimed that evidence of phosphorus poisoning was found in Edward. That substance was also available in rat poisons and could have been administered in small doses for a long time, as well. The prosecutor's opening statement in the Kufahl trial also says poison "of an arsenic nature" may have been used, leaving room for yet another form of induced ill health.

As was constantly emphasized in the trial, Myrtle always stuck to her story, once she had revised her original confession, that it was Kufahl who actually mixed the strychnine.

Still, one woman who knew Myrtle at the time, Clara Howell Pierce, author of *Historical Gleanings of Melendy's Prairie*, stated matter-of-factly when recalling the events that the common wisdom around Whitewater was that "she [Myrtle] put a little [poison] in every now and then so he went downhill slowly." Clara Pierce was eighteen that spring, and her aunt was a friend of Myrtle's. The young Clara was often taken along to visit at the Schaude home and so was quite familiar with the family.

The afternoon before Edward's death, Kufahl became even more daring in his approach to Myrtle. While assisting her as usual in the kitchen, he suddenly bent over and kissed a mole on the back of her neck. Myrtle said she asked him if he was crazy, and he answered, "I didn't do anything, I just kissed your mole."

Kufahl did admit that he had a relationship with Myrtle, although he claimed she instigated it. But he was far from the innocent farm boy he made himself out to be, and other people would agree with Myrtle's teasing assessment of Kufahl as "crazy." Ed Messerschmidt, who knew Kufahl later in life, described Kufahl as "about the oddest duck you ever saw."

Whether he was odd, crazy, or truly criminal, one thing about Kufahl was certain. He had no compunctions about demanding the affections of a married woman and taking actions to compromise her reputation right under the noses of her husband and children. And he seemed to have found a married woman who at the very least tolerated his attentions, luckily for him and unluckily for Edward Schaude.

# Chapter Five

## Strictly Strychnine

It's amazing, looking back at murder histories of the past two centuries, to learn that strychnine was not discovered by modern society until 1818. It was a product that received almost immediate public acceptance both for its lawful purpose as rodent remover and for its secondary, unlawful usefulness as a human being remover. Records show it had become one of the poisoner's primary weapons of choice by the mid-nineteenth century. *(See the early 1880s tale of the murdered sister of a Whitewater typesetter in Chapter 1.)*

Arsenic, a chemical also used in the killing of rats and humans, had been known since ancient times. The fairly easy availability of both arsenic and strychnine as rodenticides in newly industrial America doubtless added to the popularity of both substances. But strychnine had a few advantages over arsenic. It didn't leave those telltale white lines and horizontal ridges on the victim's fingernails, and it disappeared from a corpse's insides more rapidly. And strychnine, like arsenic, also had medicinal uses in very small doses. Despite its extremely bitter taste, it performed well as a tonic and stimulant when mixed in the correct (minute) quantities, so that its existence in a home could be explained away by several reasons.

Strychnine comes from the seeds of the ominous-sounding nux vomica plant, of the genus *Strychnos*. (Another famous *Strychnos* plant product is curare, the poison used by Amazon tribespeople on their arrows and blow darts.) It is an alkaloid with a crystalline structure, and about two milligrams per pound of body weight will dispatch a rat quickly. Humans require an average of one hundred milligrams for fatalities to occur, though as little as thirty milligrams has been known to do the job on a smaller person.

When someone is overdosed with strychnine, its stimulant qualities explode, causing extreme agitation of the central nervous system and spine. It takes only about five minutes for the muscles to start to twitch and the victim to begin experiencing difficulty breathing. Sometimes within just an hour an overdose of strychnine causes convulsions similar to those of tetanus or lockjaw, causing the facial muscles to grimace in what has been called "the grin of death." But the convulsions, painful as they are, don't actually kill the victim. Death comes from paralysis of the respiratory center in the brain's medulla, making breathing impossible.

The presence of strychnine may be detected by treating residues with a few drops of sulfuric acid, which will turn the substance purple. And luckily for intended victims in these modern times, neither arsenic nor strychnine is generally used in rat poison anymore since the invention of other chemicals. (Arsenic was also made harder to obtain when old-fashioned arsenic-coated flypaper was outlawed, thereby preventing people from boiling it and skimming the chemical residue off as many clever poisoners learned to do.)

It's hard to say how many people have died from strychnine in the past century and a half, but newspapers and true crime almanacs are full of both strychnine and arsenic cases. The poisoners often are women. That's logical, because women would have traditionally handled the food and drink. Was Myrtle inspired by media reports of role model murderesses? Although the Whitewater murder of Annie Horan happened a few years before Myrtle was born, there was another well-publicized strychnine murder in Wisconsin in 1891, which Myrtle may have been aware of and which bears some strange similarities to her own case history.

August Derleth wrote about the death of Ella Maly of Richland Center in his book *Wisconsin Murders*. Ella was killed at the age of twenty-three by another young woman in town, Rose Zoldoske, who was said to be jealous of the local doctor's supposed affection for Ella. The not-so-sweet Rose had already poisoned the doctor's wife, hoping he would find her an acceptable substitute.

To rid herself of Ella, too, Rose threw a party at which she schemed to send some chocolate cream candies stuffed with strychnine home with Ella and her sister, Lillie. Luckily Lillie wasn't hungry, but Ella dutifully ate her candy so as not to waste it and very quickly felt ill. Doctors were called but were too late to save her. Before she died, Ella herself thought of and mentioned the similarity between her symptoms and those of the doctor's wife.

Rose was indeed brought to trial for both murders and found guilty, despite her protestations of innocence. The townspeople of Richland Center defended her vehemently enough to inspire a scathing editorial against them in the *Madison Democrat*. After all, reasoned the townspeople, Rose was far too pretty to murder anyone. And although Rose was sentenced to life in Waupun Prison, she wangled a pardon from the governor after only eight years, a feat that would be bested by another pretty murderess a few decades later.

But back to Edward Schaude on his sickbed … at the age of fifty-one, there was no indication that Edward had been a sickly man before taking ill. Sickly men don't rise daily at the crack of dawn to milk a herd of cows, bottle all the milk, load it in a wagon, and deliver it all over town, then come home and wash out the milking equipment and containers. In addition, he possessed a robust singing voice, often booming his favorite hymns around the house. It was doubtless puzzling to him when he began to develop gastrointestinal problems in early spring. But according to his obituary, he kept singing his favorite old hymns daily through his illness, when he had the strength.

Edward's illness started almost exactly two months after Myrtle's mother, Caroline, died unexpectedly while paying a visit to relatives in Jefferson County on January 6, 1922. Caroline collapsed while putting on her wrap to leave, so she may have had a heart attack or stroke.

It's hard to say how her mother's death would have affected Myrtle. She doesn't mention it in the letters of hers that are preserved, or in her court testimony. It seems, though, that Myrtle's family was close, because she often mentioned that her sisters were visiting. And newspaper accounts of her trial paint a picture of a very supportive father and brother physically holding her up to hear the verdict. At the very least, though, her mother's death could have turned Myrtle's thoughts to death and morbidity in general and would not have been a positive thing in her life.

On top of her mother's death, the little daughter of one of Myrtle's sisters also passed away just a few days before Edward did, in another county. Myrtle's father had just traveled there to pay his respects to his granddaughter at the time Edward met his Maker.

Myrtle admitted in court that she never told Edward about her conversation with Ernst about how Ed might "croak" soon. And she noted that Edward appeared weak and exhausted for two weeks before taking to his sickbed. After Edward had been unable to get out of bed for about a day and a half, Dr. Charles E. Dike was called to have a look at him. It was then that Dr. Dike diagnosed Edward's problem as "yellow jaundice" and "catarrhal inflammation of the stomach" and left both tablets and liquid medicine for him. Powdered bismuth to be used as a sedative was one item he later remembered prescribing for Edward.

Myrtle said she told the doctor Edward had been asking for prune juice and asked whether it was all right for him to have it. Dr. Dike told her yes, and so she provided it, straining and boiling the prunes herself.

Dr. Dike paid Edward a second visit in a couple of days and examined a portion of his patient's copious vomit, which Myrtle had saved. The material was bright green, prompting the doctor to inform Edward that he was "vomiting up his gall," never a good sign. Today doctors would be more likely to call the substance "bile." It's a digestive fluid the body stores in the gallbladder to be released into the small intestine when food is present, and strong vomiting can sometimes cause it to regurgitate into the stomach where it can then be "thrown up" for a variety of causes. Edward had been doing some serious retching.

Myrtle said she always held Edward's head and the slop jar, too, as he was "in such pain" every time his insides emptied. She had to be keenly aware of Edward's utter, wretched suffering. When Edward was able to rest between vomiting episodes, Myrtle said she either sat in the rocking chair or lay down on the davenport in the adjacent parlor, ever alert to Edward's symptoms.

This had been going on for days, and it was evident that Edward was doing poorly, to say the least. And yet, Dr. Dike told the family he thought Edward was getting better on that second visit. Perhaps Edward had purged most of whatever was ailing him. That may not have been what Myrtle wanted to hear.

Just a couple of days later, on March 17, Kufahl came back from classes in midmorning as usual and helped Myrtle wash out the empty milk bottles collected that day from the route. Delbert and Ralph were probably making the deliveries before school; they had previously taken turns helping their father on his route every morning.

The milk bottles had to be washed in the milk house, which was "quite a little distance" from the house, and water first had to be carried from the house. Kufahl helped Myrtle carry the water down, and then he told her that he would be at the house in case Edward needed anything. He stayed there half an hour, she said, before he came back to help her finish up, and the pair walked back together. Kufahl was there in the house with Myrtle all afternoon, too, wiping the dinner dishes, mopping the kitchen floor, and helping her catch up on the ironing. He also offered to sit up with Edward that night, said Myrtle, but Edward understandably preferred the company of his wife to that of the odd ex-soldier.

Once Myrtle and Kufahl were alone again in the kitchen, their mood was anything but somber, considering that the mole-kissing episode happened then, with sick Edward lying in bed on the other side of the kitchen wall.

At some point, said Myrtle, Kufahl told her he would "mix some medicine [for Edward] to deaden the pain and make it easier, so [she could] get some rest." She said he then put some prune juice in a cup and took the bottle of strychnine down from where she kept it in an upper cupboard. "Just as he took it down, I says, 'Ernst, that is poison.' He says, 'All medicine is poison, don't you know that? I am only going to fix it enough to deaden the pain.' He shook a little into the prune juice and told me I should give it to Mr. Schaude when I went to bed. He set it back up on the top shelf, back with the strychnine."

Later, after supper, Myrtle said Kufahl peered at her face and said she looked tired. "You needn't keep telling me about it," she snapped. And then, she said, Kufahl began dancing around, hopping on one foot, singing, "You will get some rest, get some rest, get some rest, get some rest tonight," as he carried the dried supper dishes back and forth to the cupboard.

The *Wisconsin State Journal* blared this little song-and-dance routine in their front-page headline February 15, 1924. "WOMAN BLAMES LOVER FOR MATE'S MURDER, Pranced About After Preparing Poison," it read.

Because Kufahl did deny the dancing or even knowing about the poison, Myrtle might have made up the story. She made herself very believable, however, with all the conversational details. And, even when questioned very closely in court concerning not only what was said but about the exact placement of all rooms and furniture in the house and where she and all parties concerned were in relation to the house at various times, she never made a misstep in her testimony. Kufahl, after all, did have a vested interest in seeing Edward gone. There was an attractive woman and a farm, to boot, in the potential deal for him.

But it was Myrtle, not Kufahl, who purchased the strychnine at Duffin's Drug Store in Whitewater, just before Edward began getting sick. She bought it at her husband's request, she told the clerk, because he had forgotten to buy some to take care of rats in the granary. She paid seventy-five cents for a small, corked bottle and then mixed it with some cornmeal and placed little dishes of the mixture "between the feed barrels, under the pig trough, and in the corner by the bobsleds." She claimed those were the places Edward had told her to put it. Myrtle estimated she still had half a bottle left after baiting the barnyard rats—more than enough to kill a man.

After the kitchen had finally been tidied up after supper and the poisoned prune juice sat waiting in the cupboard, Myrtle went back into the bedroom and sat down with Edward, massaging his hands and forehead until he rested. She told the court later that Edward seemed to be better that day. Earlier, Edward had even told his children he thought he might get up and get dressed the next morning. After Edward had fallen asleep,

Myrtle moved to the sitting room to do some mending, and Kufahl joined her at the dining room table, still formally dressed in his coat, tie, and stiff collar. "If I remember rightly, I think he was mending stockings too," she added, "but I won't say for certain."

The two older boys had gone out to a basketball game for the evening, and at about 7:00, Myrtle tucked six-year-old Mae and Lawrence, four, in their little bed at the foot of their father's sickbed. Kufahl sat up with Myrtle until 10:00, she said, telling her before he went upstairs to his room that "You better go to bed before you go to sleep," and then, "Don't forget to give Mr. Schaude his medicine."

Myrtle told the court she understood that to mean the prune and strychnine mixture.

Myrtle sat up another hour, and finally at 11:00 she rose and took the cup of strychnine-laced juice from its place in the kitchen cupboard and set it on the dresser in the bedroom, where Edward could reach it easily. He told her he was feeling "quieter" and more able to rest, she said.

Myrtle undressed and climbed into bed on the other side of Edward, in her normal place next to the wall, a change from the past several nights, which she spent sleeping in the parlor. Edward rose to relieve himself in the slop jar after Myrtle laid down, and she said after that she went right to sleep, not even waking up when Delbert and Ralph tiptoed into the house after their basketball game.

It wasn't long before Edward awakened her, though, as he raised himself up to sip his prune juice. "He says, 'That is awful-tasting stuff,'" said Myrtle, "and then he took a drink of water and then he laid down again, and I went right to sleep again." Myrtle had brought two glasses of water into the room for Edward, she said, probably anticipating he would want some after tasting the bitter juice.

Myrtle didn't sleep long this time either (if she really was able to sleep knowing her husband had just swallowed strychnine). Edward woke to say, "Myrtle, I feel so funny, my toes are getting stiff." Myrtle crawled to the foot of the bed and began rubbing his toes, but Edward told her that hurt and that he was getting stiff in the knees and feeling "queer."

Myrtle started to rub his legs. "I could feel the muscles and cords twisting, and I knew that was not right," she said. She claimed she got out of bed and tried to call the doctor but that she couldn't get the city's central switchboard, which was disputed later in court.

The clerk on duty in the telephone office that night, a Miss Nelson, testified that she remembered the night very distinctly because there were many calls made after Mr. Schaude died. She said she handled all of those, was very alert, and would have known if any calls came in before the one where Myrtle actually did get through to Dr. Dike. There were no prior calls, she insisted. Furthermore, the phone company manager told the court he inspected the "telephone apparatus" the next morning, and it was in mechanically perfect condition.

Myrtle said after her first "try" at calling the doctor, she returned to the bedroom just in time to see Edward begin to convulse. "He begun to holler with pain," she said, "and I got up on the bed, and started to rub him, and he begun to sweat. And I says, 'You will feel better now you are sweating.' He says, 'Get the doctor, or it will be too late.'"

Myrtle claimed she again tried to reach the operator but couldn't, so she threw on some clothes and woke up Ralph, asking him to ride to Dr. Dike's house on his bicycle. Frank Brettschneider came downstairs with his trousers pulled over his pajamas to see what the commotion was, and then Kufahl followed him down, still completely dressed in his coat, tie, and collar. Delbert, the second oldest son, had also awakened, and he was asked to take his little brother and sister upstairs and put them to sleep in his bed.

Myrtle claimed she tried a third time to get the operator with still no response, so off Ralph hurried. There was another doctor in town who lived closer to the Schaude family, although his office was farther away, but it didn't seem to occur to anyone that it might save time to get him instead of Dr. Dike.

Meanwhile Edward had gone into a final spasm. "He just seemed to stiffen right out; his head went backward," she said. Frank Brettschneider and Kufahl were standing near the bedroom door, and Myrtle asked Frank to help her rub Edward. Frank complied, massaging Edward's lower legs while Myrtle worked on Edward's chest and arms. Kufahl, however, came only as far as the doorway and declared the scene made him "sick to his stomach," then he retreated back into the parlor. Myrtle said she told Kufahl to try to get the doctor but didn't know if he tried or not. If he did try, the phone company had no record of it.

Edward managed to ask for some water, and Myrtle raised a glass to his lips, but Edward's muscles were too tight for him to drink it. "His back seemed to raise up in the middle," she recalled, "and his stomach came up. Then he seemed to quiver and tremble all over, just seemed to shake. And he had quit sweating when he got over to the front of the bed, and he had his elbows resting on the bed, and his fingers were outstretched and stiff, and kind of curved in at the ends, and he seemed to fight with his arms, or throw them, and bring them up; and he seemed to be quivering all over. As I was rubbing him I noticed how hard his muscles were," she continued, "they seemed so hard and extended. They seemed to bulge out and all I could think of was a baby in a spasm. That is the reason I thought Ed was in a fit; I thought Ed had got into a fit."

Next Myrtle noticed Edward's eyes becoming glassy in a fixed stare, as his pupils dilated in a classic end-stage symptom of strychnine poisoning. His last words were, "Oh, Myrtle."

She still tried to get some water in between his teeth with a spoon, but the jaw was already completely set. "I thought, as I looked at him, that he must have suffered with pain somewhere, because he looked so set," she noted astutely, having absorbed every detail of his travails with clinical precision. Evidently it finally seemed hopeless enough to make her decide she could quit, because she left the room again and at last reached Dr. Dike on the phone just as Ralph arrived at the doctor's home on his bike.

By then Edward was probably dead, although Myrtle said she didn't know it until Dr. Dike came about twenty minutes later and told her so, sometime between 1:30 and 2:00 in the morning on March 18. The doctor, seeing there was nothing he could do, fetched Myrtle's neighbor, Mrs. Tim Moriarty, from across the road to come and sit with the newly bereaved widow. And it wasn't long before Rev. Allen Adams and his wife showed up to comfort Myrtle too, and finally, of course, came the undertaker (and town mayor), George Coppins.

Dr. Dike had left for the evening by the time George Coppins arrived, but they both admitted later that they thought the same thing upon seeing Edward's grotesquely contorted body: poison. They had each seen plenty of people die from influenza and gastrointestinal disorders. The Spanish influenza had passed through Wisconsin only four years earlier, providing many such examples. Edward's condition didn't fit the profile.

But how would Edward have been poisoned? Dr. Dike explained in his testimony later that he assumed it must be suicide because, "I didn't think there would be anything else, from my knowledge, from the general condition, and the family history was another thing," he testified.

By "family history," he probably meant that just a little more than two years earlier, in 1919, Edward's older brother William had committed suicide in Nebraska, where he had farmed since leaving Rome as a young man. William was fifty years old at the time.

Dike officially listed Edward Schaude's cause of death as "influenza," to prevent what the prosecutor termed as "the rising of scandal." "I was looking out for the living," explained Dike.

George Coppins told the district attorney that he just shook his head when he first saw Edward's body. "I noticed that the eyes were open and very staring, settled back in the sockets, shrunken condition. Fists were clenched; all the muscles were badly extended and very, very rigid." This condition differed from a "normal" corpse, he added, because of "the staring condition and shrunken eyes, the clenched fists, and extended and rigid muscles." Coppins estimated he viewed the body about forty-five minutes after death occurred.

So to spare Myrtle and her children further grief, the doctor and the undertaker stayed discreetly mum. And Myrtle somehow failed to mention to either one of them that she'd given Edward strychnine just a few hours before.

Sometime during this commotion Myrtle found Kufahl standing alone in the dining room with his back to the heat register and accused him of fixing the prune juice "too strong." Kufahl replied, according to Myrtle, "'I fixed it, and I will fix you if you say a word.'"

Whether Kufahl actually said that or not, things were fixed, indeed, by then.

# Chapter Six

## In the Funeral's Wake

*"FOR SALE AT ONCE—Milk route, bottles and wagon. Inquire of Mrs. Edward Schaude, Whitewater, Wisconsin."*

—the Whitewater Register, Whitewater, Wisconsin, March 30, 1922

*"You know that old saying if you can't be good, be careful. So I guess that is what we will have to do."*

—Myrtle Schaude, letter to Ernst Kufahl, 1922

It's understandable that a young widow with four children would wish to unburden herself of a herd of dairy cattle and the chore-heavy milk route that went with them as quickly as possible after her husband's death. In order for her ad to have appeared in the *Register* on March 30, Myrtle would have needed to have placed the ad only a week after Edward's demise. There's no mention later that she had any trouble selling Edward's business, and the farm was sold, too, by the following August.

The fact that Edward Schaude left no will for his estate, worth about thirteen thousand dollars, was discovered soon after Edward's funeral. For the four days between Edward's death and his services on Tuesday, March 22, the house had been filled with family and townspeople making condolence calls, so Myrtle probably had little time to think about it. And she had other matters to decide, such as what to do with her husband's body. The family didn't own a cemetery plot, and the ground was still frozen too hard to dig a grave. On Mr. Coppins' advice, Myrtle reluctantly agreed to have Edward's body placed in a vault above ground rather than having him buried.

Kufahl, who by all accounts lurked near the family the entire time rather than discreetly going home to Watertown for the weekend, overheard Myrtle discussing the vault burial with her relatives and the undertaker. "Ernst said he didn't like the idea," said Myrtle in court later. But there wasn't much she could do about it at the time.

Rev. Allen Adams led afternoon services for Edward at a funeral home on North Prince Street, then at the Methodist Church, and afterward the family gathered at Myrtle's farmhouse. Both of Edward's parents were dead by then, and one of his sisters lived in Nebraska, but his other sisters would have been there, along with Myrtle's father, brother, sisters, and their families. They probably all wondered about the keen interest Kufahl showed in Myrtle's affairs. Myrtle's brother, Frank Coad, was definitely keeping a sharp eye on Myrtle and Kufahl, as the following court testimony shows.

Myrtle said in court that after the funeral, she had been sitting in the dining room with her family when she started crying. Wanting to be alone, she went to her bedroom, which had been set up as a sort of auxiliary parlor with the bed replaced by a sofa, but Ernst followed her in and took her hand. He told her to quit crying and come back out, she said. "He says, 'You will break down and be telling something, ... you mustn't tell or you will be getting me into a nice mess.' I says, 'I will try not to tell.' He says, 'You have got to stick to it.'"

While they were having this purported conversation, Frank Coad strolled in to see what was going on and, assessing the situation, told Myrtle to go back out where she belonged. She did.

Frank was only twenty-three at the time of Edward's funeral, and he was probably one of the more interesting characters in the saga. Shortly after graduating from high school, he broke the family farmer mold and joined the Chautauqua, which was a sort of traveling, cultural university started in New York State, as a performer and violinist. He probably had to be called back to Wisconsin for the funeral. Frank never married but had as life partner a man named Lon Johnson whom he met during his stage work.

Frank Coad eventually moved to New York and worked for the Crowell-Collier Publishing Company, buying a small farm with Lon there. Unfortunately, Frank contracted some unspecified illness, which caused the two men to return to Wisconsin. They bought another small farm in Dousman near one of Frank and Myrtle's sisters, where they lived until Frank died at the young age of forty-four in 1943. His obituary said that "when Mr. Coad died, Mr. Johnson made all the arrangements, and accompanied the body of his friend to Palmyra." He was buried in the Siloam Church cemetery.

But in 1922, Frank was very much alive, and watchful. In retrospect, it's too bad that he hadn't been able to see how serious his sister was about Kufahl and convince her of her folly earlier. But that might have been impossible by this point, anyway.

A few nights after the funeral, Myrtle said one of her sisters finally asked if Edward left a will, and Myrtle told her no. The omnipresent Kufahl became suddenly alert, expressing his surprise and stating indignantly that he thought every husband ought to leave a will so his family would be provided for. Myrtle had her insurance papers and other documents in a box on the table, and Kufahl, looking meaningfully at the box, said, "Well, maybe he has got a joint deed that is just the same as a will." He examined the papers, said Myrtle, and must have been crestfallen at what he found. (Myrtle could hardly have invented this scene because her family was there to witness it.)

"No, it is a warranty deed," said Kufahl. "You only get your third. You have got to go through a lot of red tape, and only get a third," he repeated, as if unwilling to believe it.

Still, a third was better than nothing. After the family had all gone home and Frank Coad was back with the Chautauqua, Kufahl stayed on. Frank Brettschneider left soon after Edward's death, perhaps unnerved by all the events, and went home for a while to his parents' native country, the former Czechoslovakia. There wasn't much to hinder Myrtle and her Ernst from being together now, and just one month after the funeral, on April 25, Kufahl drew up a little document for Myrtle to sign that would end up in court eventually.

"He came down one day," said Myrtle, "and he said, 'I bet you twenty-five dollars you will be married inside of five years.' I says, 'I bet you twenty-five dollars I won't.' He says, 'Will you sign that, if I make out a statement to that effect?' and I said, 'Yes.'"

"Hereby I promise to pay to Mrs. E. J. Schaude twenty-five dollars in gold for not being married her second time five years from date April 25, 1922.

"[Signed] ERNST H. KUFAHL

"I agree with the above statement and also agree to pay Ernst H. Kufahl twenty-five dollars in gold if I am to be married again before April 25, 1927.

"[Signed] MRS. E. J. SCHAUDE"

Despite the silly bet, according to Myrtle there was still some air of melancholy about the house during that spring after Edward died. And Kufahl went ahead and did what his religion mandated to clear his own mind of the matter.

Myrtle said she was standing in her parlor one day around Easter time when Kufahl looked in on her. "He comes up to me and says, 'Myrtle, you feel awful bad, don't you?' I says, 'Yes Ernst, I just feel terrible.' He says, 'See here, you have nothing to feel bad about.' He said he had been to confession and everything was cleared away. He says, 'Just brace up, you have got plenty of means.' I told him I rather not have a cent, and have Ed back."

If Kufahl really did go to confession, it would seem likely that he had something on his mind that needed "clearing away." It seems an unlikely detail for Myrtle to have thought up by herself, at any rate.

At the end of April, Kufahl transferred to the Wauwatosa County Agricultural School for the remainder of the semester. But he came back weekends to spend time with Myrtle, even though he admitted his folks thought it strange that he did, and even stranger that Myrtle would allow him to.

By the time those weekend visits began and possibly earlier, Myrtle had begun spending nights with Kufahl in the room that she kept open for him. The prosecution fully explored in court how this happened.

First, as soon as Frank Brettschneider had cleared out, Kufahl moved into his room and Myrtle moved upstairs into Kufahl's former space. The two rooms adjoined with a door between, which Myrtle didn't lock. Myrtle said that one night, when she came upstairs to go to bed, Kufahl put his arm around her waist and "walked her into his room." She said she didn't call for help because there was no one to help her, other than her children.

And she claimed that although she was in his bed for "quite awhile" before slipping back to her own room about 3:00 in the morning, she begged him to let her go the entire time. She wasn't able to on her own, she explained, because Ernst took her shoes and dress off, leaving her in her slip, stockings, and underwear. She said he replied, "You wouldn't want the children to find you in this predicament. What would they think of their mother?"

She also told the prosecuting attorney that she had been in bed with Kufahl five or six times after Edward's death, according to the court transcript:

> *Q: And each time you were in bed with him you were undressed?*
>
> *A: Yes, but he made me every time.*
>
> *Q: After he made you undress the first time you continued to go up to his room, did you?*
>
> *A: I never went in there of my own free will, never.*
>
> *Q: How did you come to go there?*
>
> *A: He took me there.*
>
> *Q: Where did he take you from?*
>
> *A: Sometimes he would take me from downstairs up there, and sometimes he would be at the top of the railing, and take me in there.*

Myrtle never did explain just why she felt compelled to go with him. He wasn't holding a gun to her head. (She did claim later that Kufahl indirectly threatened her with a gun.) She admitted she ate breakfast with him the morning after their first time in bed together, as if nothing had happened. She did intimate in court that he was threatening to expose her poison purchase if she didn't play along with him. But if Kufahl was really forcing Myrtle to have sex under duress, she wouldn't have had to keep inviting him back weekend after weekend.

She probably wouldn't have visited him in Milwaukee, either, agreeing to register as man and wife at the Hotel Wisconsin, which they did. The couple also traveled to Chicago and stayed at the Jackson Park Hotel. It's hard to imagine how Kufahl could have forced Myrtle to meet him that way, and indeed she never claimed that he had forced her to. Kufahl later claimed in court that Myrtle had asked him to go with her to those cities because she was afraid to stay in them alone, although he didn't say what the purpose of her travel was.

Myrtle also sent food to Kufahl every week while he was living in Wauwatosa—homemade brown bread, nut bread, fresh fruit, and other delicacies—and did his laundry when he visited. They both wrote letters incessantly.

Here are excerpts from one that was introduced in court, from Myrtle to Ernst, written while he was in Wauwatosa.

"And as for the fifty cents, Ernst, I will take it this time, seeing you want me to, but really those few handkerchiefs I washed, I like to do it, just love to wash them <u>for you</u>; and every week if you have any you want washed <u>let me do it</u>. . . . By being so <u>good</u> to me as you are, that more than pays for all I do for you. I know your little tongue is in a wet place, but it never slips too much. Mine is also. As for being good, you are good enough, and careful. You know the old saying if you can't be good be careful. So I guess that is what we will have to do. Now, dear Ernst, don't think you have to look at every word before you speak, because you don't. Now, I am wondering why you can't understand me. Well, Ernst, that must be the nature of the beast. I have been told that by many all my life. My goodness, such a long letter. I could write a lot more. Isn't it funny I can write to some people better than others. I wonder why. Ernst, I was told once awhile ago that I was too honest in my saying, wording, looks and feelings; but so it goes. I can't help that either. But I can always be careful. Sincerely, Your Little Milkmaid."

That letter alone could probably provide a psychoanalyst fodder for an entire thesis. "Little Milkmaid" likely refers to an earlier reference in the letter to a glass of milk she had poured for Ernst in which she said the cream rose to the top by the time he drank it. But probably the parts in that letter most interesting to the jury were those references about keeping little tongues from slipping, and being careful rather than good. The sentence where Myrtle describes herself as "too honest" is close to laughable, all things now considered.

In another letter written to Kufahl about the same time, Myrtle coyly asked whether it wouldn't be nice if she could bring his bath towel up every day, and signed the note, "Your Fussy Little Fairy." She always seemed to get "Little" into her signature, perhaps unconsciously illustrating that theory of poisoners as immature people who never quite grow up. Or maybe it was just her way of framing herself in the way she thought would be most appealing to her younger lover.

The postman was busy between Whitewater and Wauwatosa. In May, two months after Edward's death, Kufahl sent Myrtle a gold wristwatch for her birthday. She waited until Kufahl arrived for his weekend visit, and then she tried to return it, saying she wished she had never met him. Kufahl told her to take the words back, but Myrtle refused, according to her testimony. When he returned the next weekend, she said, he asked her to take the statement back again late one evening. When Myrtle refused a second time, Kufahl went upstairs and came back down with a revolver and said, "Now, you have got to take that back," whereupon Myrtle fainted. When she came to, Kufahl had laid her on the davenport with a cold washrag on her forehead.

After a little more conversation, she said Kufahl told her, "Now, while I hold this little weapon in my hand you have got to promise me that you will never tell what I done to Ed." She said she promised. But she had been crying, and when her son Ralph came into the house he asked his mother what the matter was, and she told him she was scared. Kufahl showed Ralph the revolver and said, "I just showed her this, Ralph, that is not anything to scare her, is it?"

Myrtle said Ralph only smiled and went upstairs. (Ralph was also a witness in court, so he may have been questioned about this.)

By June, Myrtle had found a place she preferred to the farmhouse, a bit larger and on Main Street within the city limits of Whitewater. It was a nicely appointed wooden frame home, with room for the children and boarders, too, and within an easy walk of the Normal. The trouble was, she hadn't sold the farm yet and the owners of the new house wanted a cash down payment. Kufahl at first offered to ask his "Daddy," Watertown farmer Ferdinand Kufahl, to borrow the money for Myrtle, but she wouldn't hear of it. He then offered to lend her $825, scraped together from his own savings. Myrtle took him up on that one, writing him a personal note promising 6 percent interest (she later repaid it, but Kufahl would not accept the interest) and soon moved in. She could now house eight female roomers and feed more than two dozen, probably the only way she saw to support her family.

Kufahl visited her in that house, too, even after she had taken in eight female roomers once school started again the next fall and was also serving daily meals to a "boarding club" of twenty-six to thirty Normal School students. One can only imagine what the roomers thought of Kufahl's visits.

With the coming of summer, the ground thawed and Myrtle had Edward's body transferred from the vault to a proper grave in the town's lovely Hillside Cemetery. That act seemed to please Kufahl, she said. "Later," she testified, "after Mr. Schaude was buried, Ernst was out for the week end, and we were washing the supper dishes, I think, and Ernst said, 'I am glad Ed is buried six feet under the sod; I feel easier.'" Myrtle probably did, too.

But she didn't feel easier about everything. Eventually, Myrtle discovered Kufahl was still carrying the revolver around. One evening, she said, Kufahl was in her kitchen swatting flies on the ceiling, standing on the table and then the electric stove to get at them. "He says, 'I am going to sleep with you tonight,'" Myrtle testified. "I says, 'No, you are not.' I says, 'You promised me faithfully you would never make me do that again.' He says, 'A fellow can break his promise.' I says, 'I will not let you.' He says, 'If you knew what I had in my suitcase you would let me.'"

Myrtle took no chances, sleeping in bed with one of her female roomers that night. The next day, she allowed Kufahl to take her car to visit his family in Watertown, which would have been the perfect opportunity to check his suitcase, but she didn't. She waited until he came back to ask him if he had taken his soiled clothing out of his suitcase for her to wash, and when he said he hadn't, she retrieved the dirty laundry herself. It was then, she said, that she saw the revolver lying in the bottom of the case. She didn't do anything about it, however, and Kufahl did not seem inclined to flash his firearm around much after that incident.

Although he kept the revolver with his own things, Kufahl left a few of his possessions for Myrtle to store for him, including what the prosecution called "sexology" books. They were found still in her house more than a year later when it was searched. Kufahl didn't want to take them to Wauwatosa with him, she explained, and he surely didn't want to keep them at his parents' house in Watertown. And besides, he had encouraged Myrtle to read them, and Myrtle said in court that yes, she did read them. Myrtle was nothing if not compliant.

After his year's stint in Wauwatosa, Kufahl left around the end of April 1923 for agricultural project training on a forty-acre tract of land near McGrath, Minnesota. He and Myrtle had become formally engaged the month before, in March, with Myrtle claiming that before she would promise to marry Kufahl, he had to declare to her once and for all whether he really meant to kill Edward with that strychnine. Kufahl unsurprisingly said he did not, and Myrtle consented to be his wife.

Of course, the prospect of living together was a bit difficult considering Kufahl was now residing a good six-hour drive away. His acreage to be cleared for farming was about seventy miles north of Minneapolis, just south of a forest preserve and east of Milles du Lac Lake. It was a desolate area, and Kufahl depended on the few farmers and workers nearby for his mail, foodstuffs, and the occasional ride into town. He lived in a poorly heated "garage" or shed with few amenities and often complained of the cold in early fall. He was there on a sort of apprenticeship but evidently owned the acreage because he paid for improvements and sounded as if he intended to keep it and live there.

The regular weekend visits to Myrtle's boardinghouse were a thing of the past, and so their sexual energy was channeled into long-winded letters. Thanks to Myrtle's sentimental habit of keeping everything Kufahl wrote her all in one convenient box, prosecutors were able to have a field day tracking down all the veiled and not-so-veiled references made to sexual matters. For instance, both Myrtle and Kufahl talked about his "little fellow," which was revealed in court to mean Kufahl's "private parts," being lonesome.

In their letters Myrtle and Kufahl would also underline, sometimes with four or five strokes, certain words that prosecutors said were private code pertaining to intimacies between the two. In one letter, evidently answering a question from Myrtle, Kufahl wrote her he had just taken a bath, but he had not "spilled <u>any</u>" for a long time. "I don't have my mind on such so much now days," he lamented. "It don't do me any good, so what is the use of thinking about it. The kind I would want I will not get, so I will never relish <u>that</u>, but <u>it</u> may not be half bad yet!"

Exactly what most of those underlined words meant was probably never known to anyone but Kufahl and Myrtle, but most of the letters were just monotonous recitations of every excruciating detail of their daily lives. Kufahl wrote July 8 about buying $14.25 worth of two-by-fours for a garage, plus he gave a lengthy account of his haggling with a sawmill owner for more lumber. He whined about not having an icebox or a good place to cook, how the water had to be boiled for drinking, and that oranges cost sixty-five cents a dozen. He mentioned some dessert Myrtle had sent him from Whitewater, and he signed the letter stiffly, "Sincerely Yours, Ernst H. W. K."

In early August Myrtle told her second oldest son, Delbert, to pack his fishing pole, and she drove all the way to McGrath with him to see Kufahl's place for herself. She slept in a bed with her son all but one night, when Delbert was sent off to the neighbor's house and she and Kufahl shared the bed. While burning some "papers" outside one night, they talked about how things would be if they married, and Myrtle claimed he then suggested she do away with the children. Her testimony read as follows:

"We were burning paper, and Ernst asked me how I liked it up there, and I told him fine. He says, 'We could make it go all right if it wasn't for the children.' I says: 'Ernst, we can make it go with the children. Just the other day you told me you would forget that you thought the children would bother; you would try to think all right about it.' He says: 'The more I think about it the more I think they will bother me.' He says: 'I can't stand profane language.' I says: 'They don't use profane language.' He says, 'They do.' He went on like that. So in a few minutes he says, 'I will tell you what to do: fix them like the Mister.'

"I says, 'Why Ernst!' I says: 'I will tell you one thing: wherever I am those children are going to be. Where my home is those children are going to have a home, and I am going to make a home for them.' He went on and burned some more paper, and he says: 'That would be easy.' He says: 'Just get some candy, and put some strychnine in, and give it to the children.' He says: 'Children like candy, and they will eat it quick.' And I got up and went into the garage."

Kufahl denied having that conversation, although he did write in one letter, "So you have thought of the brush and when we let the fires go out." That of course is not incriminating in itself, but it does confirm that the activity took place and that there was something significant enough about it for Myrtle to write him and for him to remark upon it also.

Soon after Myrtle left McGrath, Kufahl wrote her that he had "been a real baby" since she'd been gone. "I have felt terrible blue, ..." he wrote. "Often I would sing to myself, 'I need thee every hour.' ... I was thinking of you what you have gone thru etc. and always took it good natured. But I think that I need you worse than ever now... ." He ended with a side note that read, "Be it ever so humble there is no place like with me."

A few days later, on August 22, Kufahl told Myrtle he had received a card from Frank Brettschneider and also a letter from his former sweetheart, Miss F. (Freda) Brown. Ernst wrote that he had been "half-engaged" to Miss Brown, and that she had asked him to wait for her until she was older. She was now twenty-one, Ernst advised Myrtle, and he wondered what he should say to her. He must have been fully aware of the impact this teasing revelation would have on Myrtle. "I am going to tell her that she is too late now that I am engaged to a woman with four children. Or what would you write to her?"

Myrtle said testily in court later on that she didn't feel a man who was engaged ought to be writing to any other women at all and admitted she was vexed. It probably made her even more nervous when Ernst went on to advise her in that same letter that he thought she could "live much better and more comfortable where you are than up north here," and that she should stop and consider things before selling her house in Whitewater. Then he calculated how expensive a house would be.

"Oh. My! A house like you and I like would cost at least $4000," he wrote. Next he computed the interest and payments, fully laying out the expenses. He did throw her a bone at the end by saying, "I guess I am plumb nuts over you, as Werst [his neighbor] says he was over a jane. Good nite, Sincerely yours, Ernst."

His next letter didn't help. Evidently the question of how he would get along with Myrtle and her four children in the small quarters was much on Kufahl's mind. On August 30 he wrote the following:

"I am glad to hear that you are willing to come up here. But will the children be contented and happy here and no child will ever rule me. I will be very strict that much I can say now. No cursing from anyone will be allowed… . It would be all right if I had a few of my own here now to make it a real home."

It's hard to say how Myrtle was taking this, but it probably got her to thinking about having a few more babies with Kufahl, and whether he was really going to accept her four as his own. In another letter Kufahl wrote a week later on September 7, the prosecutors marked the following paragraph:

"Dear Myrtle, Your letter of Tuesday evening was rec'd to-day, and I am sorry that I made you feel bad and sick. Please forgive me. I wrote you once or told you that I never wanted to make you feel bad again and now I have done it anyhow. I am not sick, but I do want you when you get ready to come. I have rec'd the eats today and it all is in very fine condition. Just as tho I would get it at your place… . I do think of you very often just about all the spare time, not only when I eat the eats."

Evidently, Myrtle had sent Kufahl some money to buy furniture, and he wrote about his gratitude and told her not to send any more money, he'd rather she kept what she had for herself. But in subsequent letters, he kept making it plain that he had a money shortage, was planning on asking his parents to lend to him, and so forth. That couldn't have been encouraging, either.

His next letter must have sent Myrtle into a tizzy, however. He wrote the following:

"I am a bit tired of being alone, but I don't want you to rent your house to come up here. The children have it much better there than what they could have it here. Your children are much more to you than I am and I would not think much of you if you rented your house and came up here this fall. I have written just as the thoughts come to me and I will not deny it either. You know as well and better than I do that it is quite difficult to satisfy five [quintuple underscore], much more so than just one. A person who raises one after another gets more used to it than to get a houseful at once. The responsibility is what makes me stop to consider quite often. I will always be very stricked [sic] and will not allow profane language from no one."

Writing about Myrtle's oldest son, Ralph, Kufahl went on to say, "I don't care to have another man stay with me, because then I could not rest as well as now."

On Sunday, September 16, Kufahl was having a bad time with flies, which he seemed to particularly detest, and with nightmares about Edward. His letter, dated September 15, is a telling piece of communication:

"Sunday A.M. 10:40—I am all shaved, washed and dressed up—but—no way to go to church. Have been swatting flies. I don't like them around me any more than people who powder. I have not slept well last night… . I had an awful dream this morning. I dreamed that I was carrying a corpse… . Well I don't think you care to read about my dream, it was not much, only as tho I was carrying Ed on a stretcher on the streets in Watertown. Two others were carrying at the head end. It does seem funny how a person does dream sometime. I think it was because I was thinking of the farm and how we fooled around, etc., as I was boarding at your place.

"Sunday p.m. 1:05—It is quite windy out here but nice and warm. I am thinking that you are having company from Watertown [Kufahl's relatives] to-day. I ate 1/4 of that pie yesterday and another piece this noon. I found a part of a fly in it and that spoiled it all now. I will write to the folks and Sis. Amanda yet. Good bye, Sincerely yours, Ernst H.

"p.s. Gunnufsons's horses were here last Sunday and are here again to-day. Some callers Ha Ha. Do what seems best to you with the money because I will not use your money. I still owe you some the way it is, which will be paid back soon. That letter is written with pencil and would not be any good to you at all in court. I do hope that you get it tho, then you will have nothing to worry about."

Not having the corresponding letter from Myrtle, it's hard to know what the letter "written with pencil" was about, or who wrote it. Kufahl seemed to be talking about monetary things just before mentioning it, but then he often jumped subjects from sentence to sentence. It's possible Myrtle was teasing him that she had something condemning that he'd written her, and he was telling her not to bother with it. He seemed to have given thought to what would hold up in court and what wouldn't, at the very least.

And no one can be convicted of murder for having a dream, but Kufahl's eerie nightmare about carrying Edward on a stretcher through the streets of his hometown could indicate there may have been some guilt being worked out there. The dream does seem to indicate that the memory of Edward's violent demise continued to hang in the air as a persistent specter between Myrtle and Kufahl.

Overall, the year and a half after Edward's death was a time when Myrtle and Kufahl were both trying desperately to work through what had happened, woo one another, and work out a future for themselves. Being eight years older than Kufahl, Myrtle may well have been insecure about the possibility of his finding a younger woman more attractive, especially one who could bear Kufahl his own family and who didn't impose upon him the burden of raising another man's four children.

Myrtle was young and attractive enough that she should have felt confident that another suitor would come along if this one didn't work out, but evidently she had her heart set on Ernst Kufahl and no other. And whether Kufahl told her to poison the children or the troublesome thoughts roiling in her mind were enough to make her conceive the act on her own, Myrtle soon began in her methodical way to set her terrible plan in motion.

# Chapter Seven
## The Evil Candy Lady

As summer waned in 1923, the townspeople of Whitewater sweated through their preparations for the annual return of the Normal School students. August in Wisconsin is a languid, sticky time when the humidity climbs until the atmosphere feels like one all-encompassing, swollen sponge. Even inanimate objects sweat and drip. The temperatures conspire to make the misery complete, with Fahrenheit readings often hitting the nineties or above. People survived before air-conditioning by turning on their new electric fans, drawing heavy curtains during the day to keep out the fierce sun, and quaffing lemonade by the gallon.

The atmosphere inside Myrtle Schaude's head couldn't have been any less oppressive. Just back from her trip to McGrath and a stolen night in Ernst Kufahl's bed, with all their conversations about how her children would fit (or not) into the marriage still turning in her mind, at some point Myrtle hit upon the idea that things would work out best if the children just weren't around. The letters Kufahl kept sending to hint at his second thoughts about the children and at the renewal of interest from an old flame ensured that Myrtle wouldn't forget about the topic and just hope for the best.

But as time passed, with the coming of September, cooler temperatures, and the return of Normal School students, it's surprising that Myrtle's plans didn't cool, too. It wasn't as if she had nothing else to think about. She had her new house to keep and a "boarding club" of more than two dozen young women to feed lunch and supper to. She advertised rooms for rent and took in several young women as roomers, so there was almost always someone besides her own children in the house. She had plenty of time to reconsider.

Yet on Friday, September 14, Myrtle visited Edward's grave and then went shopping. The first item on her list was a new bottle of strychnine, the old one having been used up on Edward.

Thinking it might not be prudent to raise a pharmacist's suspicions, she avoided L. A. Duffin's this time and went to a different drugstore, O'Connor's. O'Connor's advertised itself in the *Minneiska* yearbook as "The Normal School Store," with "Everything in School Material, Kodak Supplies and Confectionery." Myrtle could have bought candy there but didn't. Best not to make the connection so apparent.

Next on her agenda was a visit to the J. C. Coxe Grocery Store, which also sold candy. Coxe advertised in the college yearbook, too, boasting "A Large Assortment of Candies Always on Hand." There she selected chocolate bonbons with cream centers, one for each of her children. She secreted both purchases in her bedroom dresser, and that Sunday night she wrote a letter to Kufahl, telling him how expensive potatoes were at the groceries in town and that she planned to send the children on a drive to the country next week to buy some more cheaply.

In that letter, Myrtle also made the strange statement, "Ralph and Delbert will have some new winter clothes, and all that goes with them, shortly." She didn't say anything about the poison or the candy in that letter to Kufahl, but her confession later was extremely matter-of-fact as to what she meant to do with them.

> *"I took the candy and strychnine home and on Wednesday afternoon, Sept. 19th, 1923, about four o'clock, I went into my bedroom and took the candy and strychnine with me. I took a knife and opened each bonbon and put some strychnine in it. I fixed a piece of candy for each of the four children. After I did this I wrote a note to Professor Cotton and asked him to let the children take his automobile and go out into the country after some potatoes. I sent this note over to Mr. Cotton's house with one*

*of the children. It was my intention then to ride with the children for a little ways and give each of them a piece of this candy in which I had put the strychnine. . . .*"

—confession of Myrtle Schaude, September 22, 1923

Professor Cotton was a young, very popular instructor of "Public Speaking and Debating" at the Normal School. He and his family lived just a few houses away, on the corner of Main Street and Tratt, and Myrtle was doubtless well acquainted with them. Little Lucille Cotton was a playmate of Myrtle's daughter, Mae.

The reason Myrtle gave in court for wanting to use the Cotton's car was that her own sedan was getting a battery charged by the auto mechanic. Of course, local speculation later agreed that Myrtle figured she would keep her own car this way; Professor Cotton's loss be damned. Myrtle might lose all four children, but she would still have wheels.

The Cottons kindly consented to do this favor for their widowed neighbor, and the whole plan might have gone into action that Wednesday evening but for one complication: Ralph did not want to drive the Cottons' car. He wasn't used to it, he objected, showing unusual restraint and good judgment for a teenage boy. Perhaps Myrtle thought it would seem too odd if she insisted, so she didn't and waited instead until Friday when she would have her own car back.

On Thursday, perhaps getting nervous about her plan and needing to throw her energy into something, Myrtle rearranged her dining room and decorated it with flowers from her garden. Lena Yakes, a Normal School student who lived in a big house across the street with three other young women from nearby Elkhorn, was a part of Myrtle's "boarding club," and she noticed how different the room looked that evening.

"That particular night, she had the whole living room and dining room set up, and the tables were all different. We always had four or six people at a table, but she had long tables and that night had special flowers," said Yakes years later in a phone interview she gave at the age of ninety-three. The flowers must have been a welcome sight, because that Thursday was a "dark, dismal night," according to Yakes. And it was almost as if she and her friends had a premonition that something unusual was in the air. "The four of us were all joking when we came across the street that night that we wished something exciting would happen," Yakes said. She could have had no clue how their wish would be granted.

Yakes remembers Myrtle as a "nice-looking person" with dark eyes. "She usually stayed in the kitchen while we ate. I thought her cooking was very good and liked everything she put on the table," said Yakes.

Yakes was equally impressed with Myrtle's housekeeping skills. "I was a farm girl, and coming into town, her house looked very nice to me," she said. "Everything was nicely manicured around the place. The furniture was more or less dark, and the place was always neat and clean. She had pictures of her children standing on a table, and we always wondered about her husband. We always went past the cemetery on our way between Whitewater and Elkhorn and wondered what ever happened."

Because the young women always went home to Elkhorn on Friday, their Thursday meal was the last dinner they would eat at the Schaude home. By the time they returned next Monday, "Myrtle's Boarding Club" was permanently closed.

There is no mention of whether the next day was still dark and dismal, but perhaps the weather was nicer because Mae was out playing with her friends Lucille Cotton and Doris Duffin Wise after school. Wise, who was about eight years old that September and lived around the corner on South Prince Street, has strong memories of that Friday, and of Myrtle.

"I remember her as kind of a passive person, never very much life to her," said Wise. Wise had also played with Mae Schaude when the family still lived in their farmhouse a few blocks away. She remembered seeing Edward Schaude, too, during his illness there, and that he seemed to her a "very slight, pale man." Mae took young Doris into her father's sickroom while he was in bed there, said Doris. "Otherwise he wasn't in evidence very much," she said. "I never saw him and the children in proximity."

Mae and Lawrence Schaude were always clean and dressed adequately, said

Doris. "Like the rest of the kids," she added. "Mae and Lawrence were blond. Myrtle was a small person; she always looked very nice. I think I liked her well enough, but I don't remember her as being very involved with her kids."

Doris remembered her feelings the night of September 21 especially well. "I was invited to go along on the fateful ride when the poisoning was to occur," she explained. "Mae had invited me and Lucille Cotton, but our mothers wouldn't agree to it. I'm sure Mrs. Schaude didn't want any witnesses. I was kind of put out that I couldn't go."

Myrtle must have been itching to get the deed done, but again it was Ralph who determined the timetable. Trying manfully to help out with the family finances after losing his father, Ralph had taken an after-school job at a local butcher shop. He wasn't able to leave work and go on Myrtle's supposed potato run until his chores were finished, so Myrtle fed the youngest three their supper and then drove to the shop to pick up Ralph around 7:00.

The butcher had been busy that day. Myrtle, Delbert, Mae, and Lawrence waited outside in the car for an hour until Ralph was finished with his chores, then all drove back to the house so Myrtle could grab the poisoned candy from her dresser and drop it in her pocket, while Ralph probably washed up and changed from his butchering clothes. They finally took off, with Ralph at the wheel, at about a quarter to eight. In late September, it would have been quite dark by then.

Potatoes in town were too expensive, Myrtle told the children, so they were going to buy some at a farm. She rode with them about two blocks, to the edge of town, then asked Ralph to stop by Bert Gray's house on Main Street. Again, her own confession tells it best.

> *"When we reached there, I gave each of the children one of these pieces of candy in which I had put the strychnine. At the time I gave them the candy I knew that the strychnine was in it. At the time I put the strychnine into the candy I intended to give it to the children. I knew that the strychnine was poison and that it would kill the children. I knew this at the time I put it into the*

*candy, and I also knew it at the time I gave the candy to the children. I don't know why I put the strychnine in the candy for the children. I can't tell you at this time why I did it."*

—confession of Myrtle Schaude, September 22, 1923

Children in the 1920s were not as inundated with sweets as are most children of today, and the chocolates would have seemed a wonderful surprise to the four Schaude youngsters. They must have received the candy with gratitude, probably thinking what a kind mother they had. Myrtle instructed them not to eat the bonbons until the car had passed well into the countryside. Then, she calculated, they would soon go into spasms, the same rigid seizures she had watched Edward endure, and Ralph would crash the car. If the strychnine didn't kill them, the accident would.

It must have seemed a perfect plan. There were no seat belts or child-safety seats then, so the children's helpless bodies would fly around inside the car, perhaps even land twisted on the ground, and no one would question any odd positions or facial grimacing. It would be only natural that the children's eyes and mouths would be open with the shock of the crash, people would think. No one would suspect that Myrtle had engineered the tragic occurrence or that the children had overdosed on strychnine. How sad, people would say. First losing her husband, and then all her children in this horrible accident. Pity the poor widow.

Perhaps Ralph, working at the butcher shop through the dinner hour, hadn't had any supper. Maybe the children hadn't had any sweets in a long time. Or maybe just being children, they let their mother's request to wait go in one ear and out the other. But they all bit into the candy at once, while Myrtle stood watching in horror at this unexpected turn of events.

Ralph swallowed a piece almost whole, so quickly that it took a second for the bitter taste to sink in. He made a noise of disgust, exclaimed that the candy was bitter, and threw the rest of his piece out the window into the ditch. Myrtle realized her plan wasn't going to work; although Ralph might have eaten enough to put him into convulsions, she couldn't be sure he would die right away. If he lived through the car crash he could tell investigators what his mother had done. If Ralph didn't get a fatal dose, then the others must not, either.

Reacting swiftly, Myrtle yelled, "Don't eat that, it's poison!" Delbert and Mae had barely nibbled at the outer layer of chocolate and gave their pieces to Myrtle. The biggest worry was little Lawrence, who had just started to swallow his. Myrtle quickly stuck her finger in his throat and dug out the piece that was on its way down, then wiped out his mouth with her handkerchief.

It's unclear whether Myrtle realized at that time just how much Ralph had swallowed. At any rate, she told them to drive on and get the potatoes; she still wanted to make a call on the Grays. Myrtle might have thought her plan was completely foiled at that point, or she might have been hoping Ralph had swallowed enough that he would still crash the car. But she testified about it this way:

"As quick as I handed it to them I thought: 'Oh, what am I doing?' I hollered as quickly as I could. Ralph had already bitten his, and so had the baby. I didn't want to kill those children, I loved them; I really do love them. I want them. I don't know why I did that. It was not because I didn't want them. I tried so hard to get that candy away from them."

Lawrence was sitting in the front seat next to Ralph, and Myrtle got into the backseat with Mae and Delbert. She claims she asked Ralph to drive to the doctor, but he wouldn't. He wanted to have his ride into the country. So she got back out of the car and walked back to her house, letting the children go on into the dark countryside with their poisoned brother driving.

The failed plan must have weighed very uneasily on Myrtle's mind, as she wondered what would happen next. When she got back to the house, she took the precaution of telling the girls who roomed there that she was afraid the children had taken some poison. Her roomers were compassionate, trying to console Myrtle by taking her into the kitchen and giving *her* some candy—squares of Baker's chocolate.

Still on edge, Myrtle must have been thinking all that time. Maybe the Baker's chocolate helped, because by the time she finished it, she had come up with a tale she thought would cover her tracks. She went to the home of a neighbor, Mrs. Youngquist, supposedly to buy some tomatoes, and told Mrs. Youngquist that she was afraid her children had eaten poisoned candy. The candy came, she said, from a saleslady from a Milwaukee candy company who had stopped by that day. On her way home, Myrtle ran into Professor Cotton, and she told him the same story, even asking him to take his car and go look for the children.

In the meantime, about four miles out into the countryside, Ralph was beginning to have troubles. The strychnine was acting upon his nervous system, and his legs had gone so stiff that he could no longer control them, so that he actually drove into a ditch. Delbert, only thirteen, took the wheel, and the obedient children continued on to their destination, which wasn't far from where they were. To their dismay, no one was at the farm when they arrived, so they turned around and made for home, arriving just before Cotton was about to go search for them.

By the time they got back to Whitewater, Ralph was in a bad way. Myrtle called the doctor immediately and gave Ralph mustard water to help nullify the poison. The miserable boy was vomiting and convulsing. Dr. Dike, who had attended Edward's deathbed, showed up quickly and immediately declared a case of poison; Ralph was just lucky not to have bitten off any more than he had. The doctor was able to bring him out of his convulsions, and Ralph had recovered by the next afternoon.

Things would not be over so quickly for Myrtle. Once the doctor heard the tale of the candy saleslady, he immediately called the Whitewater police, reaching Night Marshal Addison Tubbs, who gathered some Normal School students to help look for the candy pieces still lying in the ditch at the far west end of Main Street. Dike himself went with Delbert and found the three pieces thrown out by the younger children.

Tubbs and his students found Ralph's half-eaten bonbon, already run over by a car. Dike took the candy pieces back to his office and looked at them with a magnifying glass to identify the telltale crystals. There was enough strychnine in each piece of candy to kill several persons, Dike concluded, noting how the chocolates had been cut in half and strychnine substituted for almost all the cream filling.

At first, everyone believed Myrtle's story about the candy lady. None suspected, said the September 27, 1923, *Whitewater Register*, "that Mrs. Schaude, the mild mannered and devoted mother could possibly be a party to so diabolical a plot; mothers of children telephoned to other mothers, warning them against the candy saleswoman, while efforts were made to locate her in surrounding towns."

Because it was assumed that the candy lady would be traveling around Walworth County in her dastardly efforts to poison yet more youngsters, law enforcement officials from each town fanned out to search every corner of the county that night and into the next morning. They were stymied when absolutely no one else had seen the mysterious woman. The next morning's *Milwaukee Journal*'s front-page headlines blared, "Candy Vender Hunted in Poisoning of Four Children," with a story dripping with sympathy for Myrtle.

Not everyone was buying the tale, however. District Attorney Alfred L. Godfrey, whom Dr. Dike had called to his office late Friday night, heard Dr. Dike's private conviction that Edward Schaude had died of strychnine poisoning, too, and seeing the strychnine-filled bonbons for himself, was beginning to put all the puzzle pieces together. By Saturday, he began to look a little closer to home for clues. It wasn't long before he concluded that the evil, poison-candy lady was probably no stranger but Myrtle herself. By Saturday at noon he had Myrtle Schaude arrested on suspicion of attempted murder.

Probably in shock, Myrtle was hauled to the county jail in Elkhorn while deputies thoroughly searched her entire house and talked to the roomers. One of Myrtle's sisters came to stay with the children. At about 8:00 that evening, the same time she had tried to poison her children the night before, Myrtle was "put on the grill," as the *Elkhorn Independent* so eloquently phrased it.

At first, she denied everything, so Godfrey began recounting the evidence they had found in her house. There were the three hundred letters from Kufahl, for starters. There were the leftover bottle of strychnine and cash register records from the pharmacy and grocery store. To the investigator's surprise, there were also a number of textbooks on toxicology, or the effects of poison agents on the human body. Myrtle had been studious.

Most shockingly, it appeared Myrtle had also been experimenting on rats to determine how much poison to give her children and to judge the effects. Deputies found a number of rat traps neatly put away under the basement stairs, and dishes with varying amounts of strychnine mixed into the bait. They concluded she had been trapping the rats to experiment on them, according to an article in the *Milwaukee Journal.*

"Bits of food were found scattered about the basement," reported the newspaper on September 25, "besmeared with strychnine parts which she had made and applied, but the authorities say they believe those baits of rat poison were only camouflage of the dark plot which she had concocted to destroy her children… . The investigators and the county officials believe the woman trapped the rats which came into her basement and barn with these traps, placed them under observation, and watched closely with a keen type of scientific research the effect of poisons she administered to them."

Confronted with the pile of evidence by an adamant prosecuting attorney, Myrtle finally broke. "My God, it is only too true," she wailed.

# Chapter Eight

## Dead Man Tells Tales

*"The Schaudas have always borne the highest reputation and have been especially prominent in church work. Never a shadow of suspicion has rested upon Mrs. Schauda until this affair, and those who have known her all her life are the ones who find the whole affair the hardest to believe."*

—Palmyra Enterprise, September 27, 1923

*"The attitude of the people of Whitewater particularly those who knew Mrs. Schaude, is strikingly charitable. The accused woman is 36 years old, mild of manner, pleasing of personality and with a record of kindly deeds in the neighborhood and church that had brought her high in the estimation of neighbors and fellow communicants. Not one word is said against her. Many of these people say she needs treatment rather than punishment... . The children testify to the constant devotion of their mother and lacking a motive for their destruction in so diabolical a manner, many accept dementia as an explanation... ."*

—Whitewater Register, September 27, 1923

*There sat the mild-mannered, "devoted" mother on Saturday, September 22, a prisoner in the county jail, confessing in great detail to not only the attempted poisoning of her children but to providing strychnine-laced prune juice to her husband as well. Once she started pouring forth the facts, Myrtle held nothing back except, strangely, any mention of Ernst Kufahl's part in it all. And as soon as she had finished telling what she did, she went into a "hysterical" state described variously by the newspapers as a stupor, coma, or extreme agitation.*

*"Today, Mrs. Schauda sits in Elkhorn jail, at times in a melancholy state and at other times, very hysterical, crying, 'Oh, why did I do it?'"*

—Palmyra Enterprise, September 27, 1923

Her failure to mention Kufahl's role didn't keep the feisty young district attorney from checking into the possibility that Myrtle hadn't acted alone. Alfred Godfrey's two assistants spent Sunday afternoon poring over the letters they'd taken from the Schaude home, underlining or marking any statements that referred to the couple's amorous relationship or future marital arrangements, especially where the children were concerned. Although there was no direct proof of Ernst Kufahl's involvement, there was enough material to cause high suspicion in Godfrey's mind.

Myrtle's pastor, the Reverend Allen Adams, came by the jail to console her on Sunday. Myrtle had regained enough composure to tell him even more details about what she'd been up to the past year and a half. The reverend, in turn, passed on to District Attorney Godfrey some of the facts Myrtle had confided and agreed to testify to them in court. This might seem to have been a breach of confidentiality on the reverend's part, but he would later prove loyal to his parishioner.

On Monday, Godfrey set about looking for Kufahl, somehow not knowing whether he was at that time in McGrath, Waukesha, or Watertown. Newspapermen and photographers from Madison and Milwaukee began descending on Elkhorn and Whitewater and were said to be offering as much as twenty-five dollars for a photo of Myrtle Schaude. They also offered money for photos of the Schaude children, but none of their neighbors or friends would cooperate, keeping the four youngsters protected while they were being cared for in their home by Myrtle's sisters.

The *Milwaukee Journal* already had the story on the front page of its Monday edition. "MOTHER'S TALE OF POISON PLOT INVOLVES PAIR," it read, wasting no time in bringing Kufahl into the picture. "Officials

Seek in Forgotten Past for Motive in Attempt to Kill Four Children," read its subhead. The article began with Myrtle's quoted confession to giving her four children the poisoned candy, about as dramatic a lead as any journalist could hope for. "I gave my four children strychnine filled candy as they were about to drive away into the country, believing that as the poison took effect the automobile would be hopelessly wrecked and the deaths of the children laid to the wreck," said the quote in Harry Zanders' story in the *Journal.*

Justice continued to move swiftly. By Monday evening, Myrtle was arraigned and charged with the attempted murder of her children. The only persons present were District Attorney Godfrey, Sheriff Hal Wylie, and a judge, Justice Lyon. Myrtle was ready to plead guilty to everything she'd been accused of, but Justice Lyon, assessing her mental condition and the fact that she had no lawyer, would not allow her to do so and entered a plea of "not guilty" for her.

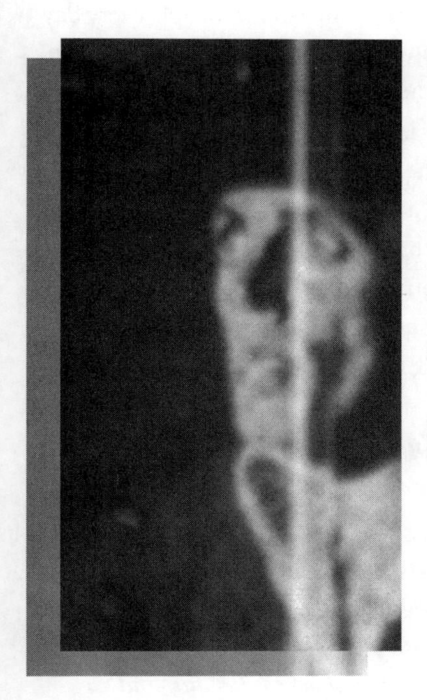

Ernst Kufahl, in Elkhorn for questioning, 1923, *Elkhorn Independent.*

Tuesday morning found Myrtle the subject of even more sensational headlines in the state's metropolitan newspapers. "WOMAN CALLED MODERN BORGIA ... Mother Who Poisoned Husband and Children Expert in Drugs," read the front page of the *Milwaukee Journal* on September 25. Evidently, the twenty-five dollar bounty had proved successful in finding a photograph, too, as Myrtle's neatly coifed image smiled sweetly above the label, "Poison Mother."

"Poison Mother," incidentally, was probably a more apt moniker for Myrtle than "Modern Borgia." Lucrezia Borgia was a fifteenth-century Italian noblewoman who developed a bad reputation for poisoning people because of the company she kept, but whom historians have since vindicated of committing any crimes. However, the article about "the Modern Borgia" went on to say investigators believed "the woman for years has been a close student of toxicology, and was better versed in poisons and their manner of reaction upon living creatures than the majority of small town physicians."

It's hard to say if that was really true. But as noted in the previous chapter, it did appear Myrtle had spent time boning up on the fine art of poison in between whipping up lunch and dinner for three dozen people every day, because she had those toxicology books in her Main Street house. The investigators had no way of knowing whether she also conducted experiments on rats while living on the Pratt Street farm, but it should be remembered that she admitted being the one to set the bait out in the farmyard, and she recalled exactly where she put each dish at that place.

The newspapers seemed to locate Ernst Kufahl in McGrath, Minnesota, about the same time as the Walworth County investigators did. On Wednesday, the *Milwaukee Journal* ran a short piece on page two titled, "POISON CASE SHOCKS VET, READY TO WED."

> *"McGrath, Minn.—Ernst Kufahl, trainee of the United States veteran bureau located on one of the Veteran Bureau projects near here, said Tuesday night that he was a suitor for the hand of Mrs. Myrtle Schaude, 36-year-old widow of Whitewater.... Kufahl declared he knew nothing of Mrs. Schaude's present difficulties beyond reports he had read in the papers. He said he expected a letter from her. He was shocked, he said, and could not believe the alleged confession or the charges lodged against her are true."*
>
> —Milwaukee Journal, September 26, 1923

It wasn't long before Kufahl was on his way to Elkhorn, driving himself by car (probably borrowed—in his letters to Myrtle, he often lamented not having a car). A sheriff's deputy had already been dispatched from

The Walworth County Jail, North Church Street, Elkhorn, Wisconsin.
*—Courtesy of Walworth County Historical Society*

Elkhorn to fetch Kufahl, who arrived at the district attorney's office at 1:00 in the afternoon on Thursday. The *Milwaukee Journal* on Friday, September 28, said Kufahl "was closeted with the prosecutor" until 1:00 the previous morning. Twelve hours is a long time to spend with a mere witness, but then there were three hundred letters to be gone over and two years of events Kufahl would have to account for. In the end, Godfrey was not willing to let Kufahl go and held him at the county jail as a material witness. Bail was set at two thousand dollars, which Kufahl was unable to furnish.

Perhaps it was knowing that Kufahl was also locked up that gave Myrtle the wherewithal to come out of her "state," or maybe it was just having had a week to think things through, but on Sunday Myrtle greatly lessened Kufahl's chances of leaving jail by declaring to Sheriff Wylie that her first confession had not told everything and that Kufahl was really to blame.

The *Elkhorn Independent* said she told the sheriff that Ernst "mixed the strychnine and prune juice which killed Ed." She also begged Wylie not to tell Kufahl she had implicated him, saying he had threatened he would kill her, too. And she also said that on the Minnesota trip, Kufahl had told her to "fix" the children as she had her husband.

Myrtle said later in her court testimony that she'd wanted to tell about Kufahl all along.

> *"On Sunday* [day after first confession] *I lay there all day feeling so terribly about that I didn't tell Ernst had done it as I should have done; thinking I would take it all on myself. I wanted to tell everyone that came near me he done it, but I was so full of fear when I thought I had to tell. I thought how he said he would 'fix me.' I thought of when he said he would make me suffer. I thought at one time how he had a gun in his hand. I don't remember much after Sunday until I came to my senses and I thought: 'I have got to tell this terrible thing,' and I told."*
>
> —Myrtle Schaude, cross-examination at her trial, February 1924

Myrtle further claimed in her testimony that her jail physician, Dr. Ridgeway, told her Saturday, September 29, that she would have to tell everything before her nervous condition would improve, and the next day, a week after she felt "so terribly" about not telling on Kufahl, it weighed so heavily on her that she had to take action.

> *"... All day, as I lay there, I couldn't raise my head from my pillow. I just wanted to tell everybody that came near me, and it just seemed as though I had something right in here I was holding tight, that just tried to get out. And I think it was Sunday night I started to tell Mrs. McCarthy, and she wanted to know if I did not want to tell Mr. Wylie; and I said yes, I wanted to tell somebody. She called Mr. Wylie, and I told him; and just as soon as I told him I felt just as if I had taken a thousand pounds out of my body."*
>
> —Myrtle Schaude, cross-examination at her trial, February 1924

It must have seemed very logical to all who heard the accusation, much more logical that an ex-serviceman and war veteran should commit murder than this demure housewife. And it could mean a lot to Myrtle. As the *Elkhorn Independent* explained, "Should later developments show that Kufahl was the engineering genius of the whole plot, as Mrs. Schaude insists he was, her sentence may be shortened to a great extent, with a possibility of a pardon at some later date."

Wylie and Godfrey didn't waste any time. The *Elkhorn Independent* noted that on that same Sunday, following Myrtle's accusation, Kufahl was grilled a second time by J. W. Page, Godfrey, and Wylie from 9:00 at night until 3:00 the next morning but would still not admit any complicity. In fact, Kufahl's reply reported in the newspapers was that Myrtle "must be insane." And yet, more information must have been squeezed out of Kufahl in his grilling than he would have liked, because the next week's *Whitewater Register* revealed that "it is said that Kufahl has talked enough to show him guilty of knowing of Mrs. Schaude's plans, particularly in the case of her husband's death."

Myrtle told county officials, said the *Milwaukee Journal*, that it was a letter from Kufahl that led to her final attempt to take her children's lives. She told of how he wrote, "If you don't hurry up with your work down there, I'll have to get another housekeeper." The word "work" was understood by Myrtle to mean committing the murder of her children.

By the next day, Kufahl's faithful family somehow raised the bail money, and his father, Ferdinand, and one sister set out to deliver it to Elkhorn on Monday morning. Justice Lyon was out of town, however, and evidently there was no other recourse because the pair finally had to go home to Watertown without their Ernst. District Attorney Godfrey had no intention of letting Kufahl leave town, anyway. The *Elkhorn Independent* reported later that week that according to "one of the local authorities," had the Kufahl family succeeded in springing Ernst from the county jail, Godfrey would immediately have served him with some other charge to keep him there.

In the meantime, Myrtle's relatives had also been busy on her behalf and had hired a pair of Elkhorn attorneys to represent her: Roscoe Luce and Charles Wilson. By midweek she was still considered too fragile to be charged with murder, however. The October 4 *Whitewater Register* read,

"The extreme hysteria which threatened her reason last week has passed but she is very weak and is being carefully nursed back to normal strength."

Luce and Wilson, of course, seized on the potential guilt of Ernst Kufahl as the most likely way out for their client. They also thought of claiming illness as a mitigating factor, but not right away. Almost two months after Myrtle's arrest, they hired a medical expert to come to the jail to examine her for mental competency, but strangely they didn't seem to think of it at the time when she was actually hysterical, while her condition was much more dramatic.

There seemed to be no end of questions for Ernst Kufahl, either. Thursday, the evening of October 4, he was dragged back into the hot seat for more interrogation, and he also met with Myrtle for the first time since arriving in Elkhorn. The meeting was not dramatic, said the *Watertown Daily Times*. "Mrs. Schaude barely glanced at Kufahl when she was led into the room where he was being questioned," it noted.

The *Milwaukee Journal*, however, had a much more interesting version of the encounter in its October 6 edition, with details provided by Sheriff Wylie:

> *"When Kufahl was led into the room where Mrs. Schaude sat, he glanced at her and hastily turned his head. She looked at him beseechingly. He halted several steps from her and took a chair facing away from her.*
>
> *"'Ernest, come over here; I want to take your hand,' Mrs. Schaude pleaded.*
>
> *"There was no reply nor any stir from the man who sat rigidly staring into space.*
>
> *"'Ernest,' she pleaded, 'why don't you tell the truth? I have told them the truth and I wish you would.'*
>
> *"Still there was no response from the rigid man.*
>
> *"Mrs. Schaude dropped her chin upon her bosom and began to weep softly. She refrained from a hysterical display of her grief, however. Jail attaches say she is composed now and displays none*

> *of the hysteria that marked her constantly for several days after her arrest.*
>
> *"'I am guilty,' she says frequently, 'and I want to take my punishment.'"*
>
> —Milwaukee Journal, October 6, 1923

On Friday, October 5, Kufahl was formally charged by District Attorney Godfrey with mixing the poisoned prune juice, with aiding Myrtle in murdering Edward, with acting as an accessory before fact in the murder of Edward Schaude, and with inducing Myrtle to give the poison to Edward.

But now that the prosecution had both Myrtle and her lover safely behind bars, there was one more witness to call forth: the late Edward Schaude. He couldn't speak, of course, but the remains of his body might prove more eloquent than any speech if evidence of poison was found in them. Kufahl's previous relief at knowing Edward was "six feet under" must have turned to extreme trepidation once it became plain what the district attorney intended to do.

On Saturday, October 6, shortly after noon, the grave of Edward Schaude in Whitewater's lovely Hillside Cemetery was opened and the coffin raised to the surface. State pathologist C. H. Bunting had planned to take the body to the Coppins Funeral Home to use the "undertaking" facilities there but, according to the October 11 *Elkhorn Independent*, changed his mind for some reason after the body was exhumed. Instead, two sawbucks and three planks were hastily thrown together at the graveside, and the body was examined right there in the cemetery, in the open air.

State chemist Clarence Mulberger had made a trip from Madison to assist Bunting in his task, and the pair worked for more than two hours to examine Edward's heart, lungs, stomach, brains, and other organs. At the examination's end, Edward Schaude's body, aside from the few pieces taken to Madison for laboratory tests, was set back in his coffin and returned to its final resting place, not to be disturbed again.

The results of the postmortem were not immediately conclusive. Bunting could not find any organic problem or evidence of sickness among the remains, and the only abnormality of any organ was a slight congestion in the lower part of the bowel, which the doctor said could have been caused by phosphorus poisoning. "No trace of effected organs," declared the *Elkhorn Independent*, "shows that Edward Schaude died from some cause other than sickness. This result in the examination is exactly what the authorities in the case were looking for," the paper continued, "although the result appears to be damaging to the state case."

But the testing was not over. The chemist, Mulberger, had taken his samples from the corpse back to Madison for evaluation, and it would take him three weeks to obtain the final results. "Strychnine poison has been detected in the stomach of a dead man even as long as six years after burial. It is that form of poison that the authorities are looking for," continued the *Independent*, "and if he met death through this form of poison it will be found in the tests at Madison."

The November 8 edition of the *Elkhorn Independent*, which announced that Kufahl was bound over for a circuit court trial in February, seemed to confirm that the tests were positive.

> *"The fact that Mr. Schaude was poisoned was established by state pathologist, Dr. C. H. Bunting of Madison, after he had made an examination of the organs from the exhumed body of Mr. Schaude. This was brought out during the cross-examination of one of the witnesses, Dr. Charles Dike, of Whitewater, at the hearing on Saturday. Dr. Dike testified that he had received a report from Dr. Bunting, of Madison, and that contained in the report was the result of the examination of the internal organs of Mr. Schaude. Strychnine poisoning was found in the stomach and intestines in sufficient quantities to cause death."*
>
> —The Elkhorn Independent, November 8, 1923

There could no longer be any doubt that Edward Schaude had not died from normal "stomach ailments." It looked like his grisly disinterment and examination had been worth the trouble in seeing justice done.

# Chapter Nine

## Widow Tells All

As undertakers and state examiners made their solemn procession into Whitewater's Hillside Cemetery to have a look at the remains of Edward Schaude, they met with the cemetery caretaker, or "sexton," as such workers were then called, and learned another intriguing fact.

As mentioned earlier, on the morning Myrtle made her trip downtown to buy bonbons to disguise the rat poison she planned to feed her children, she also took flowers to Edward's grave. The bouquet was still there as proof, lying withered in front of the headstone, when Edward's body was exhumed. "The wilted petals, still clinging to frost-blackened stems, hung dejectedly from the cup at the base of the headstone, as mute testimony to this last ceremonial," said the October 6 *Milwaukee Journal*.

What was Myrtle thinking? Was it a token of appeasement, in her mind, to Edward's spirit for what she was about to do? Was she trying to tell him that their four youngsters would soon be along to join him in the next world? Or was it just a carefully planned detail to make her appear the grieving widow and keep herself beyond suspicion?

Of course, by the second week in October, Myrtle's intentions regarding the graveside flowers were now beside the point. Both she and Kufahl continued to languish in, as the *Elkhorn Independent* put it, "the county bastile [sic]" across North Church Street from the courthouse.

Myrtle was attended at all times by a nurse as she continued to regain her strength. The district attorney, of course, was eager to proceed with hearings in both cases but was sufficiently convinced of Myrtle's illness to keep postponing them. Godfrey was determined that Kufahl's hearing should go before Myrtle's, evidently believing he had a better chance of convicting Kufahl that way.

On October 13, a week after Edward's body was raised, the report from Madison seemed to provide enough evidence for poisoning that Kufahl was formally arraigned. But his case was continued until October 27 on the grounds that Myrtle was not able to appear in court until then, and her hearing was scheduled for October 31. The *Milwaukee Journal* reported in their October 13 edition that Kufahl, not surprisingly, "seemed disappointed at the delay."

"This means two more weeks in jail," Kufahl stated glumly as deputies led him back to his cell. Sheriff Wylie replied astutely, "You're lucky if it is only two weeks." Kufahl, of course, wasn't that lucky. As October 27 neared, officials decided Myrtle needed at least one more week, and the hearing was postponed again until 9:00 on Saturday, November 3. As news spread the next week that this time the hearing would proceed, the populations of Whitewater and Elkhorn were abuzz with the prospect of finally learning the sordid details of the affair and murder. The townsfolk would not be disappointed.

Myrtle was led across the street that frosty November morning in her winter coat, a heavy fur collar tucked up around her face to shield herself from the throngs of curious onlookers and reporters as well as the cold. Sheriff Wylie supported her on one side, Deputy Sheriff Margaret McCarthy on the other.

Once at the courthouse, she had a little time to prepare herself while George Coppins, Whitewater's mayor and undertaker, gave his testimony "largely to prove corpus delecti," according to the *Milwaukee Journal.* As Myrtle removed her heavy overcoat, necks craned to see what the notorious widow chose to wear in her first public appearance. Myrtle, as all the newspapers noted, was indeed fashionably turned out. She wore a blue-gray, beaded skirt; a sheer, blue and gray checkered crepe de chine blouse, or "waist," as it would have been called then; and white silk stockings with gray suede pumps trimmed with black leather. She topped the outfit off with a brown silk hat, adding only her wedding band for jewelry.

Not that Myrtle was exactly parading herself. The *Delavan Enterprise* said she had to be carried to the witness stand, apparently having "lost the use of her lower limbs entirely, due to the nervous strain she has been under." The paper added, "She was pale and her eyes were sunken from her sickness and incarceration in the county jail here, but in spite of these blemishes her beauty was apparent to all."

Once ensconced in the witness chair, Myrtle leaned to her right and rested her chin on her right hand, with her fingers partially covering her mouth so that she constantly had to be admonished to move her hand in order for the judge to hear what she was saying. She kept her eyes on the floor and never looked at Kufahl sitting with his attorneys, Skinner and Thauer of Watertown and W. C. Zabel, Milwaukee.

She would be followed by two other witnesses, Dr. Dike and her former neighbor Mrs. Moriarty, but the *Delavan Enterprise* said that of the witnesses, Myrtle provided most of the "sensational testimony." She endured three hours of cross-examination altogether; one in the morning and two more after the lunch break. "Her testimony was for the most part of an unprintable nature," said the *Delavan Enterprise*, "and she bared her soul as to her relations with the defendant, Ernest Kufahl. Details so sordid were brought out under the cross-examination, that many of the spectators left the crowded court room before her examination was completed."

The same details given in a courtroom today, of course, would probably not cause most people to blink an eye. But those were different times.

Kufahl remained unemotional while Myrtle recounted her story, keeping his eyes intently on her from less than fifteen feet away. He was also nattily dressed. The *Elkhorn Independent* described his wardrobe as consisting of a dark blue serge suit, white shirt and collar, a knit tan "four-in-hand" tie, and black shoes. "He was clean shaven and somewhat pale from his long stay indoors," said the paper. "His dark hair was parted on the left side and combed straight back. His appearance was pleasing, and he would be considered to be fairly good looking."

Myrtle seemed able to keep her emotions in check, too, although she hung her head whenever the questions came around to her relationship with Kufahl before Edward was poisoned. She had to admit that Kufahl put his arm around her waist and kissed her in the barn, and also through the glass of the kitchen window. She told how she made the eggnogs for him and took them to his room to be sure he got his eight to ten glasses of milk a day.

But this was nothing compared to what Myrtle was forced to reveal about what went on after Edward's death. The *Elkhorn Independent* called it "one of the most sensational hearings in the history of Walworth County." None of the newspapers dared print the tale of Myrtle's seduction and subsequent dalliances with Kufahl at the time of the hearing, but it's a safe bet that the gossip grapevine was ripe for the picking around Whitewater and Elkhorn after those attending the hearing revealed what was said.

> *"The high point in the examination from the view point of the court room habitues was reached when Attorney Zabel of Milwaukee, Kufahl's lawyer, pitilessly interrogated Mrs. Schaude who for the first time in two months had left the county jail, and was there as a witness. She admitted she and Kufahl were lovers, denied improper relations although admitting that at times, after her husband's death, she had brought food to Kufahl's room while scantily clad."*
>
> —Whitewater Register, November 8, 1923

A hush fell over the courtroom, said the *Watertown Daily Times*, when Myrtle came to a "recital" of the killing of Edward Schaude, stating flatly that Kufahl mixed the fatal dose of strychnine into the prune juice, and divulging all the details of her husband's death throes. The *Milwaukee Journal* noted, "Her testimony about her affections for the soldier, who was a boarder in their home, was given in a hushed, hardly audible tone, but her answers to questions about her husband's death were clear and louder."

All the papers noted that Myrtle came closest to "breaking down" when asked about the attempted poisoning of her children. Under the title "Hangs Head at Admissions," the *Milwaukee Journal* described it this way:

*"When W. C. Zabel, attorney for Kufahl, questioned her about attempting the death of her children, she hesitated for nearly a minute before replying that she did attempt to kill them with poisoned candy.*

*"The woman told how Kufahl, a Whitewater Normal School vocational student, became a star boarder, intimate friend, and then, after her husband's death, lover. She hung her head when she admitted they were lovers.*

*"Mrs. Schaude said she dumped the contents of the strychnine bottle [used to kill Edward] into the sink and washed it down about three months after her husband died. Then she threw the bottle across the street.*

*"'You knew you would have further use for it, didn't you?' asked Mr. Zabel.*

*"'No.'*

*"'But you had to buy more for your children, didn't you?' asked Mr. Zabel.*

*"'Well I did buy more.'*

*"'What pain were your children suffering that you had to deaden by giving them strychnine?' demanded the lawyer, and the woman was silent, with bowed head."*

—Milwaukee Journal, November 4, 1923

At times, said the *Elkhorn Independent*, the cross-examination by Zabel became "extremely sarcastic." "Upon one occasion," said the *Independent*, "his remarks became so caustic that he was reprimanded by Justice Williams and the spectators applauded, which called for use of the gavel to restore order."

Zabel also repeatedly accused Myrtle of involving Kufahl because she was afraid another woman would "get" him, but she denied that. "The lawyer asked if Kufahl did not send her a letter received by him from another woman, and whether Mrs. Schaude did not write back that the letter annoyed her," said the *Milwaukee Journal*. "She acknowledged it was true," it continued. "The widow admitted sending Kufahl a $25 check as a birthday gift and also giving him $20 or $25 when she went to Minnesota to visit him. She admitted sending him food 'dozens' of times."

Myrtle also told the court that Kufahl lent her $825 for the purchase of her house and would not take any interest when she repaid him.

Zabel, evidently a skilled interrogator, also forced Whitewater's good Dr. Dike to admit that he believed Edward was killed by strychnine all along, and to confess that he knew he was "signing a lie" when he made out Edward's death certificate ascribing the cause as "influenza."

The state finally rested its case about 4:30, at which time Zabel formally requested Kufahl's release. Justice Williams immediately denied the request, binding Kufahl over for trial. He would have another "long stay indoors."

On Tuesday, November 6, the *Milwaukee Journal* ran a huge photo of Myrtle's face, complete with graphic frame embellishment, on its front page. The caption read, "Cries for Her Babies." The short paragraph below read, in part, "She cries for her babies to whom she is alleged to have fed deadly drugs."

Of course, Myrtle's hearing was still to come. And on Saturday, November 15, Myrtle was secretly taken to Whitewater and arraigned there before Justice Williams on the charge of first-degree murder. Myrtle pleaded not guilty, and a hearing was set for the next Saturday in Elkhorn at 9:00. Myrtle was brought to Whitewater for her arraignment, the *Whitewater Register* explained, "in order to give her a brief outing" since she had been confined so long in Elkhorn. Her entourage included Sheriff and Mrs. Wylie and the ever-present nurse, Anna McCarthy.

Myrtle's hearing was not nearly so hard on her as Kufahl's had been. She was present in the courtroom but did not testify. Kufahl was not called as a witness, either. As the *Elkhorn Independent* noted, "The hearing was marked by the lack of sensational testimony which was so rampant in the Kufahl hearing held here a short time ago."

George Coppins was called once again to the stand to testify as to the condition of Edward's body when he prepared it for burial. He told about the body's unnatural stiffness.

Dr. Dike was also recalled, and he repeated the statements he made at Kufahl's hearing. He added, however, that Myrtle did appear very much grief-stricken and upset after her husband's death.

Some sparring between the attorneys added drama, as attorney Godfrey introduced damaging testimony given in the Kufahl hearing, and Myrtle's attorneys responded by introducing the entire transcript of that hearing with emphasis on the part that told how Kufahl mixed the poison and prune juice for Edward.

Next on the stand was Myrtle's minister, the Reverend Allen Adams, who managed to throw the unflappable Godfrey for a loop when he refused to testify after being called. Adams used his constitutional right allowing clergymen to refuse to testify regarding any information given to them by a parishioner, said the *Elkhorn Independent*. "District Attorney Godfrey evidently was very much surprised," said the *Independent*, and "stated to Justice Williams, that Mr. Adams had previously volunteered certain information to him, and he had understood that the Reverend was perfectly willing to go onto the stand for the state, or he would not have summoned him."

Justice Williams ruled it a case of "privileged information," said the *Whitewater Register*, and the reverend was allowed to step down. According to that newspaper, Adams said later that "the necessity of answering 'yes' or 'no' without a qualifying expression promised to create a false impression and rather than have that occur, he chose to fall back on his rights as her pastor."

Sheriff Wylie was the state's next witness, called to tell how Myrtle confessed to both the attempted killing of her children and to the killing of her husband. The defense then induced him to also tell the court that Myrtle was "nervous and excited" when she made her confession, and about how she went into the "coma or stupor" immediately after. The defense also went to great pains to note that she came out of the stupor after making her second statement implicating Kufahl.

The final witness was a deputy sheriff of Walworth County, Mrs. George Harrington, who was present when Myrtle was arrested and at her confession. "Mrs. Harrington corroborated Sheriff Wylie's testimony regarding the confession and arrest," said the *Elkhorn Independent*, "and stated that Mrs. Schaude did not tell of the details of the poisoning of her husband, but merely said, 'Yes, it is all too true,' when asked if she had poisoned Mr. Schaude."

Harrington also noted that she thought that Myrtle was "very apparently in her right mind and in full possession of her faculties" when she made these statements.

Confronted with that devastating testimony, Justice Williams refused attorney Wilson's request that Myrtle be dismissed, and he bound Myrtle over for trial along with Ernst Kufahl. The trials were tentatively set for February's term of court, and Myrtle was sent back to her cell to languish.

She wasn't alone, however. The November 30 *Elkhorn Independent* noted that many arrests had filled the Walworth County Jail to capacity.

> *"In the auxiliary cell room on the lower floor may be found Mrs. Myrtle Schaude, principal in the Whitewater poison case. She is attended at all times by Mrs. McCarthy of Eagle who acts as nurse. A late report states that Mrs. Schaude is improving steadily and that she is at present able to walk a few steps alone. Her condition at the time of the hearings in this city will be remembered by a great many."*
>
> —Elkhorn Independent, November 30, 1923

# Chapter Ten

## The Delicate Jailbird

Life behind bars is seldom a pleasant proposition. It's even less so at holiday time, of course, especially for people who are accustomed to big family celebrations. However, as November rolled into the Christmas season at the jailhouse in downtown Elkhorn, Myrtle Schaude and Ernst Kufahl were not forgotten by their families or the public.

From newspapers of the time, it's evident that the good citizens of Walworth County were themselves in the thick of Christmas preparations. In Elkhorn, the new Methodist Church advertised a bazaar to be held on December 12 featuring homemade mincemeat. The editor of the *Whitewater Register* somberly reminded, "those of you who are to carve a duck on Christmas day that the celebration is primarily a religious one and that all mention of the deity must be made in the proper spirit." The paper also announced that "Herr St. Nicholas" would be visiting the city on the night of the Community Christmas Tree program, with bags of goodies for every child attending.

District Attorney Alfred Godfrey was busy frying another big fish, one Adolph Eckman, Darien, who was on trial for the murder of Carl Fritz after the two tussled over a shotgun and Eckman won. Godfrey successfully nailed a first-degree murder conviction in Eckman's case, which was almost as well publicized as Myrtle's. The *Whitewater Register* wrote, "District Atty. Godfrey, by his speedy conviction of Eckman, tried last week for murder at Elkhorn, demonstrated that he is familiar with the dodges often resorted to by legal talent to free a client and can be trusted to forestall any such actions to the end that justice shall prevail. His handling of his first murder case is a great credit to him and the *Register* does not hesitate to offer its congratulations."

(Eckman appealed his case, and two years later, in 1926, Alfred Godfrey again represented the state against Eckman, this time opposing Chicago attorney Clarence Darrow! Godfrey won his case a second time, even with Eckman's high-powered defense.)

Doubtless, Myrtle Schaude and Ernst Kufahl were both aware of Eckman's first trial and its unhappy outcome for the defendant. Eckman was also confined to the county jail until his transfer to prison could be made, and he would have served the pair as a constant reminder of their own impending days in court. Holiday cheer was probably in fairly short supply in the jail as Christmas approached.

Still, the December 27 *Elkhorn Independent* noted that the prisoners in county jail "spent as happy a Christmas day as was possible under the circumstances." Most prisoners were allowed to receive packages of presents such as candy, fruit, and books and were visited by family members.

Myrtle received "a number of packages," the *Independent* said, and was paid a call by two of her sisters and "one of her younger children." Whether Myrtle didn't wish the older ones to see her in jail, or they just hadn't quite gotten past her poisoning their father and trying to kill them, too, is hard to say. The older boys would certainly have been aware of her confession by then.

Kufahl also received many gifts from friends and well-wishers and spent the day with members of his family who made the trip from Watertown.

Even convicted murderer Eckman was joined by kith and kin.

The prisoners were also served a delectable Christmas dinner of roast chicken, dressing, mashed potatoes, gravy, cranberry sauce, dessert, and coffee. And to top off the day, Elkhorn pastor A. B. Bell brought his church choir to entertain the inmates with a vocal and instrumental Christmas concert.

The day after the holiday, harsh reality returned as several convicted prisoners were shipped off to state institutions to begin serving their sentences, another fact that probably didn't escape either Myrtle or Ernst.

No mention is made of how the prisoners rang in the new year of 1924, and January probably seemed a tediously long month as they awaited February's resolution of their fates. On January 24, the *Watertown Daily Times* insisted Kufahl was a model prisoner, spending several hours each day reading from the Bible to his fellow prisoners. It also said that Myrtle was still in ill health. The article said Kufahl's defense team was preparing itself well, with local attorneys Skinner and Thauer again to be joined by Milwaukee's W. C. Zabel.

At the same time, it said, District Attorney Godfrey and his partner Jay W. Page were steadily gathering their evidence against the former lovers. The paper speculated that because of the notoriety of the case, it would be very difficult to find jurors untainted by pretrial publicity.

As the trials grew nearer, Kufahl took a brief furlough from the jail one day when a deputy sheriff accompanied him on a short walk to a nearby menswear store where he bought a new suit, said the *Watertown Daily Times*. "Kufahl talks little, but maintains his innocence," added the paper.

Nothing is written of Myrtle's personal preparations for trial, but it can safely be assumed her sisters were visiting often and taking care of her wardrobe arrangements as well as her children.

The lawyers and defendants were not the only ones preparing for the trials. On the week before Kufahl's trial date of February 11, the *Whitewater Press* listed a group of witnesses subpoenaed to appear at both trials. It included Myrtle's two oldest sons, Delbert and Ralph; her neighbor Mrs. Tim Moriarty; Whitewater's mayor and undertaker George Coppins; Myrtle's pastor and his wife; Dr. Dike; and Dr. Dunn. Also listed were housecleaner Mrs. Gertrude Wagener [sic] and neighbors Mrs. Herbert Taft, John O'Brien, Mrs. Anna O'Brien, Mrs. Eleanor McGowen, and Miss Ethel Upham (perhaps a boarder at the Schaude home).

Potential jurors were also being called to Elkhorn. A total of thirty-six were asked to report the next Monday, in order to ensure enough of them to come up with a solid group of twelve.

The weather, almost as if reflecting the mood of the trials, was terrible. The first week in February brought a big snowstorm with gale-force winds that left Whitewater residents without electrical power. The roads between Elkhorn and Whitewater, about fifteen miles altogether, were not the well-paved highways they are today, and many jurors and witnesses planned to stay overnight in Elkhorn rather than brave the snowdrifts in their lumbering automobiles. It was appropriate that the Methodist Episcopal Church in Whitewater would list as their first hymn for the next week, "From Greenland's Icy Mountains."

The weather would stay that way throughout the trial period, too. At one point, the road was so completely blocked that Whitewater jurors and witnesses had to return home via an almost absurdly circuitous route by taking a train to Janesville, then to Fort Atkinson, and finally back around to Whitewater.

Nonetheless, it wasn't the weather but Kufahl's defense team that caused a delay in the trial. As court convened Monday with Judge E. B. Belden presiding, Kufahl's lawyers filed an affidavit of prejudice against Belden. The case was adjourned to Wednesday, February 13, and it was expected that Judge C. M. Davison would make the trip from Beaver Dam to preside on that day.

Kufahl's attorneys, said the *Watertown Daily Times* in its February 12 edition, were "determined to exhaust every possible means to delay the trials of the Watertown world war veteran until after Mrs. Schaude's case has been disposed of." District Attorney Godfrey was equally set in his insistence that Kufahl should be tried first. Attorneys Zabel, Skinner, and Thauer knew, of course, that if Myrtle should go first she would almost certainly be found guilty due to her confessions, so that they would have a much easier time getting Kufahl set free. The *Elkhorn Independent* also speculated that the lawyers figured they would gain insight into the prosecution's case if Myrtle's trial was forced to precede Kufahl's.

As things turned out, Godfrey's wishes prevailed. When Beaver Dam's judge was unable to make it, Judge C. A. Fowler from Fond du Lac was called to serve, and Ernst Kufahl's trial began on the afternoon of Thursday, February 14. Despite all the dire predictions from the local press about the difficulty in putting a jury together, most of the required jurors had been found the day before, ten of them farmers like Kufahl and his family. Still, the first panel of thirty-six was exhausted and two additional panels of twenty were required before a jury both sides could live with was finally assembled on Thursday morning.

There weren't any women on the jury, a fact that might be explained by the following passage that ran several weeks earlier in an area paper:

> *"There were a couple of nasty cases on the calendar at the county court this week and a corresponding exodus of women jurors, all of whom became suddenly indisposed or had to get home to do a washing. We don't blame them."*
>
> —Whitewater Register, December 1, 1923

Although that was printed well before the Kufahl and Schaude juries were selected, it does show the mind-set of the local women of the day. It's likely a sudden, great obligation to laundry chores arose again when the women called to serve at Myrtle's and Kufahl's trials thought about judging the salacious stories that were now common knowledge around Walworth County. It was simply too embarrassing to be officially associated with such things. But attending as spectators was another matter, and there was no shortage of female observers at either trial.

A less determined court might well have been cowed into further postponements, but it was obvious that the local officials were anxious to get the Schaude show on the road.

"Not only is there great local interest in the trials this week at Elkhorn of Edward [author's note: error, should have read "Ernst" rather than "Edward"] Kufahl and Myrtle Schauda," said the *Whitewater Press* on February 14, "but these cases are regarded as among the most remarkable in criminal trials."

And so the most remarkable proceedings began.

# Chapter Eleven

## He Said, She Said

*"The opening scene of the final act in the notorious Schaude poisoning case, a drama that has attracted nation-wide interest, started in Elkhorn this week with the opening of the February term of circuit court and the trial of Earnest Kufahl, alleged accessory to the crime, and clandestine lover of Mrs. Myrtle Schaude, Whitewater poison widow."*

—Elkhorn Independent, February 14, 1924

Judge Chester Fowler knew Kufahl's trial would be a sensational event. Ruling that the delicate ears of minors needed protection from this testimony, he allowed only adults in the courtroom. The exceptions were Myrtle's sons Delbert, fourteen, and Ralph, sixteen, who were appearing as witnesses.

The courtroom was filled to overflowing, said the *Watertown Daily Times*, which noted the judge had to clear the aisles to make way as the jurors went out for recess and meals. Many women in the crowd of spectators brought their sewing, and most refused to leave at lunchtime for fear of losing their seats. Kufahl, sitting in the front of the room in his new suit, was the object of much attention from both the crowd and the press.

The *Times* described Kufahl as "almost cheerful, with his father and sister with him in the courtroom. He looks tired and worn, but that appears due more to his physical condition than to worry." It went on to say that Kufahl expected to be acquitted and that he insisted if he were convicted, he would enter jail "an innocent man."

As for Myrtle, there was no need for her to be carried to the witness stand as she had been during the hearings in November. After sitting with the sheriff's wife in the back of the room while waiting to be called, she walked to the chair under her own power. Her attire this time was far more understated than the sheer blouse and beaded skirt she had worn for the hearings. Still well dressed, she now looked much more the part of the widow in a simple black dress edged with jade green piping. Covering her dark hair was a small black hat, which the *Milwaukee Journal* said was "turned back to show all her pale face."

District Attorney Alfred L. Godfrey.

The *Elkhorn Independent* declared that Myrtle appeared to be a "different woman from the broken, hysterical wreck who told the sordid details of her unholy love for the defendant last fall at the preliminary examination." It also made the judgment that "instead of the thin, dark and sunken eyes, she apparently had regained some of her previous beauty."

As the prosecuting attorney, Alfred Godfrey had the first turn. In his opening statement, he brought out "many points heretofore unmentioned," said the *Elkhorn Independent*, and stated his intention to prove it was Kufahl who had mixed the poison that Myrtle administered to her sick husband.

Godfrey described how Myrtle and Kufahl sat in the living room together after Edward had been given his strychnine-laced prune juice, with the door to Edward's bedroom closed. He said that Kufahl went to bed about 11:00 but did not undress. He also told of the couple's written agreement not to marry for a certain time and how they had loved each other on the sly since 1921.

It must have shocked the spectators all over again to hear how Myrtle and Kufahl "fondled and caressed each other at every opportunity, even before Mr. Schaude's death," and that the pair shared the same room "night after night" afterward. As Godfrey put it in his statement, "Mr. Kufahl had Mrs. Schaude from time to time in his room in a nude condition." He mentioned, too, their trysts at the Hotel Wisconsin in Milwaukee and the Jackson Park Hotel in Chicago. Godfrey also made sure the jury heard how worried Kufahl was about Edward's body being placed in an easily accessible vault rather than underground. Of course, the crowd was waiting to hear things from Myrtle's own lips. When she took the stand, the spectators eagerly leaned forward to hear her every word, noted the *Milwaukee Journal.* Godfrey began quietly, by asking Myrtle about her married life, and Myrtle replied that she was happily married and that her children, when they each came along, were "very welcome."

Courtroom sketch of Myrtle Schaude by Claude "Mud" Eames, editor of Elkhorn Independent, 1924. —*Courtesy of Eames family*

The testimony's tension level escalated, of course, as Godfrey had Myrtle recite the circumstances of Edward's illness—how she placed the teacup filled with prune juice and strychnine on the dresser by his bed the night of his death, and that she saw him drink it, a fact that she had earlier denied. Godfrey brought this inconsistency out in the open, probably hoping to defuse its later use by Kufahl's defense team. Myrtle then recounted every detail of Edward's death throes as she had in the hearings, describing his agony impassively.

Next came the story of how Ernst Kufahl came to be a boarder at her house, all the little kitchen chores he did, and how he often had access to the cupboard where the strychnine was kept. Myrtle took special care to say that on the day Edward died, Kufahl took the little bottle of strychnine, removed the cork, and shook some into Edward's prune juice. Godfrey had Myrtle demonstrate for the jury, the *Milwaukee Journal* said, "with uplifted hand and shaking fingers," how Kufahl allegedly sifted strychnine from the small vial.

Myrtle's testimony stretched on into Saturday, as she recounted Kufahl's strange little hopping dance and all the other circumstances surrounding Edward's death. Godfrey drew her out in every detail, probably hoping the wealth of information would be enough to convince the jury that she was telling the truth in all matters. It would have to be enough, if Kufahl were to be convicted. After all, it was Myrtle who purchased the poison, Myrtle who placed it in her cupboard, Myrtle who admitted giving Edward the fatal drink, and Myrtle who watched him gulp the bitter potion.

Of course, all of Kufahl's attentions to Myrtle from the first months he lived in her house were expounded upon. Myrtle even admitted she wrote him a letter signed, "Lovingly, Landlady" while he was in Watertown for Christmas vacation, only a few months after he first moved in with the Schaudes. She told of how they slept together after Edward's death and how Kufahl threatened her with his revolver.

> *"He helped me up, and took me onto the davenport in the parlor, and he took the revolver out of his pocket and he says: 'Now I am doing this because I love you,' he says, 'and you have got to promise me ... you have got to tell me you will take back that you wished you had never met me. Will you do it?' I says, 'I*

> *will take it back.' He says: 'You must say you will love me.' I told him I would try to love him... . He says 'Some of your friends don't like me, and you have got to stick up for me.' He says: 'I want you. If you are going to love me you must promise you will do all you can for me.' I promised him."*
>
> —Myrtle Schaude, testimony at Kufahl trial

Myrtle's final statement under her examination answered Godfrey's question as to what Kufahl said to her before they each went to bed on the night Edward died. "Just as he was going upstairs he said: 'You better go to bed before you go to sleep, and don't forget to give Mr. Schaude his medicine,'" said Myrtle.

At that, Godfrey turned Myrtle over to Kufahl's attorney, Zabel. The *Watertown Daily Times* said that Myrtle "braved W. C. Zabel's cross-examination ... in much the same unemotional manner that she testified on direct examination, except she broke down with references to the poisoned candy, and when Attorney Zabel bared her indiscretions with Kufahl."

But it would be poor strategy to upset the witness right away, Zabel knew, so he began gently, asking Myrtle how old she was. She answered she would be thirty-eight in May. How old was Edward when he died, Zabel wanted to know. Myrtle replied that "Ed" was fifty-one. He then asked Myrtle if she knew how old Kufahl was, and she replied yes, he would be thirty-one in June.

Godfrey objected to this line of questioning as not a proper cross-examination, and Zabel changed direction. He asked Myrtle whether Kufahl and her other boarder, Frank Brettschneider, paid the same rent, and she said they did. He asked whether they both performed the same chores to help around the house, and she had to admit that Kufahl did a lot more than Brettschneider. Zabel also induced her to confess that she never told her husband about any of Kufahl's improprieties and that she never slapped Kufahl's face or ordered him to leave the house, either of which would have been the expected response to such insults from a lady of the house at that time.

Most newspaper accounts pointed to that last admission as a very damaging bit of testimony ... to Myrtle, of course, not Kufahl, although it was his trial.

Zabel took it further, forcing Myrtle to recount exactly what she was wearing—a slip, stockings, and underwear—the first time Kufahl pulled her into bed with him after Edward's death, and how she didn't get her clothing back until she went into Kufahl's room to make his bed the next day. She was in his room until about 3:00 a.m., she said, claiming that Kufahl was holding her there but admitting that she was able to fall asleep in his arms.

Myrtle said she cried, but didn't cry herself to sleep, and that she didn't "holler," either. But, she added as Zabel pressed her, she still did not call the police the next day or ask Kufahl to leave her house.

Probably one of the most distressing questions Myrtle had to answer was when Zabel asked whether, in any of the letters she wrote to Kufahl, she "in some form or another" referred to her sexual organs. She replied, head down, "Yes." Zabel then noted that his client, Kufahl, also referred to his sexual organs in the letters and added, "You have carried on quite an extensive correspondence on the subject, did you not?" Again Myrtle had to reply in the affirmative.

He also told, without contradiction by Myrtle, how she and Kufahl discussed her own sexual organs while in her home, and that they talked about sexual matters "considerably."

Zabel also brought up the "sexology" books that were found in Myrtle's house. She claimed she read some of them only because Kufahl asked her to. Zabel asked her to whom the books belonged, and she replied, "Ernst Kufahl." Zabel countered, "Isn't it a fact that they belonged to other persons?"

Myrtle did not answer.

"You saved the books?" Zabel then asked. She replied that she kept the books as Kufahl wanted her to. "Didn't burn them up?" persisted Zabel. Myrtle said no.

Zabel displayed a knack for making details of Myrtle's story that first seemed innocent appear much more sinister in retrospect. For instance, she had described how she slept on the far side of her marriage bed with Edward "because it was her place." Zabel intimated that perhaps she stayed next to the wall the night of Edward's death so that Edward could more conveniently reach for his prune juice on the dresser. He also noted that Myrtle missed a big chance to mention to Edward that he was drinking poison when her sick husband first sputtered, "It is awful tasting stuff."

Myrtle claimed that she didn't say anything because she didn't think there was enough poison in the cup to hurt Edward. Zabel easily made that claim look ridiculous.

But Zabel's biggest salvo came near the end of Friday's testimony, when he demanded that Myrtle's first confession, the one in which she did not implicate Kufahl, be produced by the district attorney for the court to see. Godfrey replied that he did not have it with him in the courtroom, and Judge Fowler told him he could give it to Zabel after the day's adjournment. "I guess we have worked the reporter hard enough," added the judge. "We will suspend at this time until nine o'clock in the morning."

Godfrey could not have been happy at this news. Showing Myrtle's original confession, with the added impact of her personal signature, would emphasize the fact that Kufahl was not mentioned at all in it. Actually, if Myrtle really had planned everything out in advance, including her defense, it's surprising she wouldn't have considered blaming Kufahl from the get-go. She had proved herself to be a meticulous planner in the way she worked out the plot to kill her children, so why wouldn't she have thought ahead to have an obvious scapegoat handy? Perhaps she really was telling the truth about feeling threatened into silence by Kufahl. That probably was what Godfrey believed, or he might not have been so eager to see Kufahl prosecuted.

Myrtle was back on the stand at 9:00 sharp the next day, and Godfrey began the proceedings by asking that the jury leave so that he could make a motion. When they were all out of earshot, he asked the judge to deny the defense their motion to introduce Myrtle's original confession. There was a lively discussion among Godfrey, Zabel, and the judge as to just how many confessions, sworn or unsworn, signed or unsigned, Myrtle really made and whether all of her statements should be made available to the court. The judge, unfortunately for Godfrey, seemed to be siding with Zabel.

"All we want is a fair exposition of everything," said Fowler. "It seems to me if the district attorney has any statements in his possession made by the defendant which contradict statements she has made on the stand, the defense ought to be given the benefit of them."

Zabel then went a little too far in pushing for the judge's permission to see everything the district attorney's office had in writing. "I do not think you have a right to paw over the district attorney's papers," Fowler admonished Zabel. But Fowler finally conceded that if Godfrey and Page had any statements in their possession that contradicted Myrtle's statements on the stand, they had to show them to Zabel. "And that ought to satisfy anybody," he added.

The jury was finally let back in.

Of course, the first thing Zabel did was ask Myrtle how many statements she had given the district attorney respecting the death of Mr. Schaude, and she replied that there were two. The second one, she said, was taken down when Godfrey wasn't present; she didn't sign it, and it wasn't read back to her. She told how she gave the second confession at the jail, first telling the sheriff's wife, Mrs. Wylie, about her accusation of Kufahl, then Godfrey, and then Captain John T. Sullivan, a detective from Milwaukee who was called in to help question Myrtle and who actually wrote down her second statement.

Another flurry of arguments ensued over whether mention of the incident of Myrtle's attempted murder of her children should be permitted, and eventually it was allowed. Zabel made effective use of it to show that Myrtle did know how to administer strychnine.

But the jury's ability to hear Myrtle's original confession probably was most damning to her, and therefore helpful to Kufahl, in their eyes. Zabel read her words, "I don't know why I poisoned my husband. I just did it." Then he asked Myrtle if that was true. Myrtle said that it wasn't true.

"Did you make that statement?" he asked her.

"I might have made the statement," she replied.

He then read a line wherein Myrtle said she understood that she was making a confession, and Myrtle said that she did not remember saying that, either. She admitted that she wasn't threatened into confessing but added that she did not confess of her own free will.

Again Zabel read, "The fact that I poisoned my husband has worn on me since his death."

"The fact my husband was poisoned has worn on me," Myrtle feebly corrected Zabel.

"Did you make such a statement?" demanded Zabel.

"I don't know," replied Myrtle.

Zabel read on from Myrtle's confession, "I am glad I have told it, and am willing to take such punishment as the Court gives me."

Myrtle said nothing.

Zabel again made the point that Myrtle said she felt safe driving to McGrath to stay with Kufahl there, and he compelled the woman to admit once more that she had "exposed her body to him." Myrtle insisted that happened only twice before her trip, however.

Courtroom sketch of Ernst Kufahl by Claude "Mud" Eames, editor of Elkhorn Independent, 1924. —*Courtesy of Eames family*

He also got Myrtle to say that she never wrote anyone a letter praising Kufahl, and then he produced two sheets of her pink, linen stationery on which she had written a letter to Kufahl's sister, Josephine, nine months after Edward's death, in which Myrtle lectured Josephine on what a fine man her brother was.

Zabel next introduced the letter in which Kufahl wrote to Myrtle that he'd received a letter from his former sweetheart, Freda Brown, and established that it made Myrtle jealous, although Myrtle preferred the term, "annoyed."

Zabel submitted other letters into evidence, including the one with the signature "Fussy Little Fairy," which several newspapers misreported as "Flossy Little Fairy."

The district attorney did not object to the introduction of the correspondence. "They are simply love letters," he said.

"That is all," replied Mr. Zabel.

Godfrey began his redirect.

His tactic was to ask Myrtle about the conversation she and Kufahl had while burning papers around a campfire in McGrath. "Did you and Ernst, as you sat there by the fire on the day in question, make up your minds that the thing you would have to do was dispose of your children?" asked Godfrey.

Zabel objected, and Fowler sustained. However, Zabel did not get his way in disallowing the subject of the couple's alleged discussion of disposing of the children altogether. "What's sauce for the goose is sauce for the gander," Fowler told Zabel. "It only has a bearing on the case, as I view it, as it may tend to show an intent on the part of one or both of these people, if they both had intent, as to giving strychnine in this particular case."

Finally, Myrtle was allowed to report her conversation while burning papers in Minnesota, when she claimed Kufahl told her to "Fix them like the Mister."

Godfrey was also able to produce the letter Kufahl wrote in which he referred to the conversation they had in McGrath when they "let the fires go out." Although Kufahl did write such things as, "You know as well and better than I do that it is quite difficult to satisfy five much more so than just one," and repeated his vow to be very "stricked" with the children, he was either cagey or innocent enough not to make any direct references to disposing of the children. And even though he seemed to be making it plain that he did not want Myrtle's brood living with them, it was not enough to persuade the jury that he wanted them dead.

Myrtle had to endure yet another recross-examination by Zabel, in which he finally produced the actual, original confession that bore her signature and made her admit that she had signed it. He then brought out her enormous lie about the candy saleslady from Milwaukee and made it seem highly suspicious that she didn't tell about Kufahl's part for an entire week.

He also read to the jury more of Myrtle's letters, about how she wished she could bring him his bath towels every day, and the one signed "Your Little Milkmaid," in which she lightheartedly repeated the old saw, "If you can't be good, be careful."

Godfrey in turn read more of Kufahl's prose: "I have been a real baby since you left. Today when I came back to McGrath my hands just shook. . . . Some men, the women have to do the leading. That is the trouble with me."

It's hard to see how that could have helped Godfrey's case in persuading the jury that it was Kufahl doing the leading where the poisonings were concerned. Godfrey promised to get more letters together during the noon hour, and he introduced five of them when court reconvened. One was the written "bet not to marry," and that was the end of Myrtle's evidence and testimony.

The trial stretched on into Saturday, and then Monday. According to the *Milwaukee Journal*, the next witness called was Edward S. Ela, a civil engineer who showed a plat of the two floors of the house in which Edward died. George Coppins was next, and then came Myrtle's former neighbor Mrs. Moriarty.

Kufahl also testified on his own behalf.

Godfrey opened Monday morning's proceedings with his best parting shot, which made a memorable headline in the *Milwaukee Journal* as, "Recalls Ghosts to Damn Kufahl." Godfrey stressed to jurors, said the *Journal*, the letter Kufahl wrote to Myrtle from McGrath:

> *"I had an awful dream this morning. I dreamed that I was carrying a corpse. . . . I was carrying Ed on a stretcher on the streets in Watertown. Two others were carrying at the head end.*

*It does seem funny how a person does dream sometimes. I think it was because I was thinking of the farm and how we fooled around etc. as I was boarding at your place."*

—Ernst Kufahl, September 15, 1923

"Is there any man among you," Godfrey asked, "who doesn't know in the bottom of his heart that Kufahl never would have mentioned to Ed Schaude's widow that horrible dream if there hadn't been a bond between them in the causing of his death? The ghost of the man for whom he prepared that deadly poison came back in his dreams to wreak vengeance upon his conscience and some peculiar tenet of justice tweaked that mind, prompting Kufahl to set down upon this page the words which give an account of that guilty dream and which enable you to remove the last vestige of doubt regarding his guilt or innocence."

The *Watertown Daily Times*, perhaps showing its bias toward hometown boy Ernst Kufahl, opined in its February 16 edition that Myrtle "blamed Kufahl for everything as if he had her under some hypnotic spell, and she was helpless in his hands."

Hereby I promise to pay to Mrs E. J. Schaude $25.00 Twenty five dollars in gold for not being married her second time five years from date April 25th. 1922 Ernst H. Kufall

I agree with the above statement and also agree to pay to Ernst H. Kufahl $25.00 Twenty five dollars in gold if I am to be married again before April 25, 1927

Mrs E J. Schaude

The Marriage Bet Contract between Myrtle Schaude and Ernst Kufahl.

The paper noted that even though Kufahl moved hundreds of miles away from her to Minnesota, she went to him there only because of his "strange influence" over her. And Kufahl, added the Watertown paper, was ready to deny all the most damaging parts. "On Friday," it reported, "he was keenly alert to all that was going on about him. He kept his eyes fastened on Mrs. Schaude and the other witnesses and wrote down many suggestions for his attorneys."

Once on the stand himself, Kufahl denied that he had anything to do with killing Schaude. He vowed, according to the *Milwaukee Journal*, that he never saw strychnine in his life before the bottle was set before him in court at the trial. Considering that he was an agricultural student and raised on a farm, it must have strained the jury's credulity to think that Kufahl had never laid eyes on what was then the most common form of rat poison, but the paper also said Kufahl was calm and appeared frank in his telling of events. Perhaps they did believe him.

Kufahl also contradicted Myrtle's testimony that he went to bed at 11:00 and appeared back downstairs hours later still fully dressed. He insisted he went to bed at 9:00, undressed, and then put only some of his clothing back on when awakened later on. (Frank Brettschneider and others later contradicted him on this and corroborated Myrtle's version.)

Kufahl also insisted Myrtle made up the story about the pistol and about his little hopping dance and song about getting rest that night. He said, too, that he never remarked he was happy at Edward being "six feet under." And he explained that he always addressed Myrtle as "Mrs. Schaude" until one day she remarked that she couldn't stand her children calling her "Ma." From then on, he called her "Ma" to tease her, he said.

Kufahl did admit asking Myrtle about the age difference between her and Edward during those months before Edward's death, when she was thirty-four and Edward fifty-one. "I said, jokingly, well you outlive Ed and then you can outlive me," said Kufahl. He claimed that he told her the only thing he didn't like about Edward was that he married Myrtle, because if he hadn't, Kufahl would have been able to.

Kufahl also admitted kissing Myrtle both before and after Edward's death and said that one time was because she "made a face at him" through the window as he was going for a pail of water. "That face should be worth a kiss," he said he told her, and so they kissed with the glass between them.

Surprisingly, Kufahl also admitted kissing Myrtle's cheek on the day of Edward's death, while he was helping mop up in the kitchen. Myrtle had said that Kufahl kissed a mole on the back of her neck. But Kufahl said that she was sitting at the table as if deep in thought, and he told her that if she came over to him, he would kiss her. She immediately got up and walked out of the room, he said, but as she went past, he kissed her "lightly." He said she then told him, "Don't scare a fellow that way," which sounds like an odd thing for a woman to say. At any rate, they did agree that there was some sort of kissing on that day.

Kufahl also had to answer for many of his own statements in the voluminous cache of his letters Myrtle had kept. They must not have been as sensational as those Myrtle was forced to confront, however. As Godfrey picked through the two large shoeboxes of letters, noted the *Milwaukee Journal*, two of the jurors "nodded drowsily and appeared to be asleep."

Myrtle was paying only slightly more attention. "As her one-time sweetheart drove home to the jurors his side of the super-sordid story," said the *Milwaukee Journal*, "Mrs. Schaude slumped in her seat at the rear of the big courtroom and softly cried to herself." She raised her head, the paper noted, only when Kufahl made his points of denial.

Alfred Godfrey also introduced a little play-acting into the proceedings when he asked Kufahl to demonstrate an incident Myrtle told about, when Kufahl said that Myrtle had taken his hand and pulled it around her waist. "Mrs. Schaude is slight and short," noted the *Milwaukee Journal*. "Mr. Godfrey stands well over six feet two inches and weighs nearly twice as much as Kufahl."

Kufahl obligingly stepped down from the witness stand and took the hand of the big district attorney, repeating what he had said he told Myrtle as he consoled her in her grief and adding Myrtle's alleged responses, too. Finally, "with great effort," he swung Godfrey around and encircled the district attorney's large waist with his arm.

That sight alone should have awakened the jury, along with providing their dose of humor for the day.

After Kufahl came a parade of other witnesses, starting with the surprise appearance of the private detective Captain Sullivan, former chief of Milwaukee detectives, who was called to identify Myrtle's second confession. Sullivan testified that he took Myrtle's second statement and that when he asked her how much strychnine Kufahl put into Edward's prune juice, she replied, "I don't know, I didn't see it."

That statement directly contradicted what Myrtle had said on the stand about watching Kufahl put the strychnine into the juice, with her shaky-handed demonstration.

Of course, Sullivan's cross-examination also revealed discrepancies between Kufahl's original statement and his court testimony, but Kufahl explained that he had denied improprieties with Myrtle at first in order to shield her.

Called next was state chemist Clarence Mulberger from Madison. Mulberger testified that he found no evidence of strychnine in Edward Schaude's body but that this was not proof that Edward didn't die from strychnine because Edward had "expelled the contents of his stomach" while in his death throes.

The state pathologist, Dr. C. H. Bunting, also testified that the condition of Edward's body prevented him from conclusively declaring a cause of death but that he believed it was due to strychnine, considering all the other facts of the case. Under cross-examination by Zabel, however, he said that Schaude's jaundiced condition might also have been due to "slow phosphorus poisoning."

Myrtle's brother, Frank Coad, pulled from his Chautauqua job in New Orleans this time, was also called as a witness. Coad said that while he was in Whitewater for Edward's funeral, he talked to the undertaker, George Coppins, about Edward's death. Coppins told him, said Coad, that his sister's husband had died from poison. Coad said he also assumed Edward had committed suicide and didn't want to upset Myrtle by telling her.

The state called C. H. Murtagh, a pharmacy student who had worked as a clerk at the drugstore where Myrtle bought her first bottle of strychnine, and Gertrude Wagner, Myrtle's former cleaning lady, who said she saw "improper conduct" between Kufahl and Myrtle while she worked at the Schaude home. Frank Brettschneider, Myrtle's other boarder, also told of seeing displays of affection between the two.

Finally, both Delbert and Ralph Schaude had to take the stand, giving their versions of the events surrounding their father's death and answering questions about Kufahl's helping around the house. It must have been extremely difficult for the boys to talk about those days, especially with their mother sitting there watching them, but the newspapers were careful to follow the lead of the Whitewater townspeople in shielding the boys from undue publicity, and nothing was written about how they looked or acted in giving their statements.

The trial recessed for Sunday, opening again on Monday for the final statements. The courtroom had a strange visitor on Monday, noted the *Milwaukee Journal.* A "mongrel" dog named Danny O'Keefe roamed the courtroom freely. Danny O'Keefe possessed the title of "Elkhorn's War Dog," since he had been picked up in France and brought back to Elkhorn by a World War I veteran to become the local American Legion mascot. "With perfect nonchalance, he nosed about the jury box and among the crowded spectators while the attorneys addressed the jurors," said the *Journal.*

The dog was probably a helpful reminder, in the eyes of Kufahl's defense, that Kufahl was himself a war veteran. It's doubtful the dog was usually allowed to roam the courthouse; he may have been brought in by Legion members attending the trial in support of a fellow veteran. It's very likely that Danny O'Keefe struck a patriotic chord of sympathy among the jurors.

Alfred Godfrey's assistant, Jay Page, began the closing statements for the state, and Zabel allowed Watertown attorney Nicholas Thauer to start their attempted exoneration of Ernst Kufahl. Thauer naturally emphasized the difference between Myrtle's two confessions, insisting that the first one she made was the only true one. He asserted, said the *Milwaukee Journal,* that evidence showed Myrtle was jealous that Kufahl might marry someone else and was resolved not to let anyone else have him.

Thauer also accused Myrtle of being the romantic aggressor, asking whether she wouldn't otherwise have cried out or protested Kufahl's affections. He also made the point that she would not have driven to Minnesota to see him if she truly were afraid of him.

Godfrey and Zabel had the final words, however. Godfrey described Kufahl as a schemer who undermined a "beautiful Christian home," and Zabel painted Myrtle as "a woman who sang in the church choir when her hands were dripping with blood."

Judge Fowler told the jury that it was obvious either Kufahl or Myrtle had "falsified," and that it was their job to determine whose testimony they believed.

He then instructed the jury that three verdicts were possible: conviction of first-degree murder, conviction for complicity in first-degree murder, or acquittal. He handed the case over to the jury at 3:02 p.m., and the jury took little more than two and a half hours to return their final ballots. The jury had voted four times; the first was nine to three for acquittal, the second; ten to two for acquittal, then eleven to one, and finally all twelve agreed to acquit Ernst Kufahl. Jurors said that the contradictions in Myrtle's story, particularly between her two confessions, were what threw the verdict Kufahl's way.

The crowd cheered.

As Judge Fowler vigorously rapped his gavel to restore order, Kufahl leaped to the jury box and excitedly shook hands with jury chairman John McFarland. Fowler ordered Kufahl back to his chair, but the crowd thronged around Kufahl, stretching their hands toward him and clapping him on the back. Kufahl then shook the hand of every juror, while his sister hugged his neck.

Kufahl's elderly father, Ferdinand, broke down and wept. "His father," said the *Watertown Daily Times*, "broken in health, stood in the center of the court room crying like a little child."

Kufahl was asked by his hometown reporter what his plans were, and he replied, "My conscience has been clear all the time, and I expected to be acquitted. Plans? Well I haven't any just now. My first thought is to go home with my father and sister, and say, haven't they been wonderful pals to me all through this?"

The *Milwaukee Journal* noted that whether or not Kufahl returned to the Silver Star settlement of farms of disabled war veterans depended on the outcome of medical examinations to determine his fitness, mentioning his "tubercular" condition and "influenza contracted in the Army."

Myrtle was not in the courtroom at all on Monday, so she was spared having to witness her former lover's triumph. Her mind was doubtlessly on the fact that she had ten counts of her own hanging over her head and would soon be back on the witness chair. Still, when Myrtle was told of the verdict, the *Elkhorn Independent* said she sobbed, "He is just as guilty as I am," then "threw herself on her cot and wept hysterically for several minutes."

Kufahl, for some reason, spent the next day not in Watertown in the bosom of his family but in Milwaukee where he was interviewed by reporters. His attitude had changed, noted the *Milwaukee Journal*. "The pitiful, pleading Kufahl of the recent murder trial, who besought sympathy from the jurors and the press row, had been transformed into an arrogant Kufahl by the acclaim and adulation of the hundreds of sympathizers who stormed the courtroom and braved the court's ire by applauding his acquittal," read the February 19 front-page story.

Kufahl's answers to the reporters' eager questions were characterized as "curt and snappy." Kufahl did tell them that he tried to see Myrtle at the jail before he left there, after packing his belongings, but that Sheriff Wylie wouldn't allow it. A reporter then asked Kufahl if he would write to Mrs. Schaude. Kufahl shouted, "No!" at the top of his lungs so strenuously that he collapsed in a coughing fit. He added that he would have nothing more to do with her.

Kufahl's father was with him on the trip, and after the press conference held at the Milwaukee railroad office, the pair proceeded to the office of attorney Zabel, probably to pay their considerable legal fee. They returned in the evening to Ferdinand Kufahl's thirteen-acre farm outside Watertown, said the *Journal*.

And, reported the *Elkhorn Independent*, the elderly Ferdinand Kufahl did enjoy one other happy incident that week, before his son's acquittal. An Elkhorn resident named Julius Opitz happened to see a photo of Ernst Kufahl in the newspaper that reminded him of an old school chum he knew in

Germany many years before. He decided to pay a call on the elder Kufahl at his rooming house in town and discovered that Ferdinand was indeed his childhood friend. "It was needless to say the reunion was a happy one," added the *Independent*.

# Chapter Twelve

## Nothing For Me But Death

> *"Whitewater sent a contingent to Elkhorn this morning subpoenaed yesterday to appear today as witnesses in the trial of Mrs. Schaude. They are Mr. and Mrs. John Youngclause, Mr. and Mrs. J. R. Cotton, E. S. Ela, J. I. Noltner, and Irma Opel. Miss Opel is a Normal student."*
>
> —Whitewater Register, February 21, 1924

After the knockdown, drag-out testimony and emotional conclusion of Kufahl's trial, Myrtle's long-awaited comeuppance seemed almost anticlimactic. On Wednesday, February 20, with temperatures hovering near zero degrees outside, Myrtle made the trip across the street from jail to courthouse one more time.

Myrtle entered the courtroom at 1:30 p.m. sharp, said the *Elkhorn Independent*, with her father, Henry Coad, supporting her on one side and brother Frank supporting her on the other. Two of her sisters, Jennie Anderson of Union Grove and Elizabeth (Libbie) Roberts of Dousman, entered soon after with Myrtle's four children in tow, and the family was seated in the middle of the room.

The paper said Myrtle "presented an entirely different appearance from the woman who had so confidently told her story against Kufahl on the witness stand here last week." Myrtle's eyes were sunken and ringed with dark circles, as if she had not slept.

Judge E.B. Belden of Racine presided over Myrtle's trial, since there were no objections to him as there had been for Kufahl's. Attorneys for both sides had already hammered out an agreement that Myrtle would plead guilty to a reduced charge of first-degree manslaughter, rather than first-degree murder as originally charged. She would also plead guilty to four charges of attempted murder in the case of her children.

The district attorney began the proceedings by reviewing the basics of the case for Judge Belden, adding that he was satisfied with the reduced charges. He rather had to be, because he had weakened the state's case against Myrtle by discrediting her first confession in Kufahl's trial. So Myrtle did still benefit somewhat from Kufahl's being charged.

Myrtle then took the stand on her own behalf, probably well aware that the wide eyes of her four children were fixed upon her. Led by her attorney, Charles Wilson, she told how her married life was happy until Ernst Kufahl darkened her door. She added that little Lawrence had his sixth birthday that day, almost to the minute of her telling it.

She was on the witness stand for two and one-half hours, according to the *Milwaukee Journal*, which said this was what might be called her "last request, before effacing her personality under a prison number, to explain without harassing the sinister story of the last two years and a half."

Every mention of the attempted poisoning of the children brought fresh tears from Myrtle this time, and at one point she "approached a state of hysteria," according to the *Elkhorn Independent*. "Oh God, I don't know why I did it," she screamed. "I loved them so ... I loved them so! I didn't want to kill those children!" She wrung her hands and writhed like a tortured animal in the witness chair, the very picture of mental agony. The *Milwaukee Journal* said that "a crumpled heap of black in the witness stand was all that remained of the woman whom spectators had described last week as so hard and so cold in her terrible recital."

Her brother Frank helped Myrtle down from the stand, and it was at this point that little Mae Schaude also burst into tears and had to be ushered from the room by her Aunt Jennie. The other children soon followed and mercifully were not in the room when sentencing took place.

Myrtle's other attorney, Roscoe Luce, pleaded for leniency, telling the judge that Myrtle had already suffered sufficiently and that he firmly believed Kufahl was the person truly responsible for Myrtle's crimes.

As was usual, Belden asked Myrtle if she had anything to say for herself, or if she knew of any reason why he should not pass sentence on her. Myrtle said nothing, just lowered her head and began sobbing. The judge performed his duty, sentencing her to ten years of hard labor at the prison in Waupun on the first charge of first-degree manslaughter, and ten years each on the other four counts of attempted poisoning. But he allowed the last four sentences to be served concurrently for a total of twenty years. The twenty years would be reduced to twelve years, six months if Myrtle earned it, he added. Not a bad punishment for causing the death of her husband, let alone trying to kill her four children.

Still, Myrtle gasped at hearing her sentence and dropped her head into her hands while Henry and Frank Coad tried to console her. "She later had to be assisted and supported from the courtroom a total physical and mental wreck," said the *Elkhorn Independent*. The *Milwaukee Journal* was more melodramatic. "Her cup of grief had not only overflowed," it gushed, "it had inundated her."

Reporters asked Alfred Godfrey if he was satisfied with the verdict, and Godfrey replied in his usual matter-of-fact way, "I am always satisfied at the end of a case. What's the use of being otherwise?"

Myrtle would have a few days reprieve before her trip to Waupun, said Sheriff Wylie. That would allow time for her lawyers to appoint guardians for the children (their aunts would take on the task, dividing the children between them) and to select an administrator for the estate. Once back at the jail, though, Myrtle fell back into a state of collapse, telling her woes to her steadfast companion, Mrs. Wylie. "It has turned out just as Earnest [sic] said it would," she sobbed to Mrs. Wylie according to the *Milwaukee Journal*. "He said if I ever told, he would deny everything and I would be the one to suffer. He is free. I am here. There is nothing ahead for me but death in prison."

"MRS. SCHAUDE IS PLEASED WITH WAUPUN— IS IN CHARGE OF THE KITCHEN IN THE WOMEN'S DEPARTMENT"

—Elkhorn Independent headline, February 28, 1924

Despite Myrtle's previous, woeful insistence that only death awaited her in prison, her pragmatic nature soon asserted itself, and it wasn't long before she was put in charge of cooking meals for the thirty-one female inmates. Her old friend from the Elkhorn jail, Mrs. Wylie, took an opportunity to visit Myrtle at Waupun when her husband, the sheriff, was obliged to transport Earl Pope of Delavan to the men's section of the institution.

The *Elkhorn Independent* reported that Myrtle told the Wylies she was pleased with prison life and happy in her "new home." The paper also mentioned that her children would soon be coming to visit her.

Myrtle also declared to the Wylies that no one had so much as spoken a cross word to her since she had been there and that she was enjoying her work as cook. She probably had kitchen helpers, which was more than she could say for the time she spent cooking for two dozen college girls all by herself. Did the other women prisoners know their food was being prepared by a convicted poisoner? Perhaps, but they wouldn't have had much choice in the matter.

The state prison at Waupun welcomed a new warden, Oscar Lee, just a month after Myrtle arrived. Lee was a reformer who believed that every prisoner should have appropriate work to occupy his or her time. He abolished standard prison punishments such as shackling inmates' arms to the wall. According to his obituary in the April 14, 1938, *Waupun Leader-News*, "He followed the thought that every man should be given a fair deal." Needless to say, Lee was very popular with the prisoners. And it's most likely that he would have seen to it that Myrtle's cooking skills were put to good use.

In fact, the *Waupun Leader-News* account of Lee's death noted that one of his first acts as warden was to have the prison kitchen remodeled into a modern arrangement with up-to-date refrigeration. As head cook for the women, Myrtle certainly would have come to his attention. He later told a reporter for the *Whitewater Register*, "I don't know what the people of Whitewater think about Mrs. Schaude but we have found her to be a mighty fine little woman." It was noted among Myrtle's prison "credentials" later that she also served as cook to the deputy warden, probably working in his home.

There was precedent for this as the warden, himself, had a prisoner as his family's cook.

Oscar Lee's grandchildren, who were contacted by the author, remember their mother telling of at least one prisoner living and cooking in her family's home. It was after Myrtle's time in Waupun, and he was a jewel thief known to the family only as "Becker." He enjoyed his work at the Lee house so much, recalled Lee's granddaughter, that as soon as his time was up, he committed another heist so he could get back to work. He had to wait quite a while before he was allowed to cook again, though.

Myrtle was a little smarter than the recalcitrant Becker was, however. Evidently she was mustering all her domestic and personal skills to get along from the moment she crossed the prison threshold, even though records say that physically she was a wreck, losing weight and unable to sleep without sedatives. And after not even one year as a jailbird, Myrtle mounted her first appeal for pardon.

Pardon docket records from the archives of the Wisconsin Historical Society show that on November 10, 1925, Elkhorn attorneys Thorson and Seymour argued that Myrtle should be released. Signing the petition in support of Myrtle's release were her sister Jennie, brother Frank, and sons Ralph and Delbert. The lawyers gathered a long list of petitions from citizens of Elkhorn, Whitewater, Appleton, and other cities, and letters pro and con were written to Governor John J. Blaine. Myrtle's cousin Mrs. E. A. Bloodgood, of Elkhorn, wrote "her family need her and want her. We all love her and have perfect faith in her."

Nonfamily members wrote, too. Warden Oscar Lee wrote, "I can frankly say that she gives every appearance of being a very fine woman, indeed, and I would in no way place any obstacle in the way of her obtaining executive clemency." Judge Roscoe Luce, Myrtle's former lawyer, wrote, "I believe that in the sight of God, this woman is innocent of the crime for which she is being punished, and that she is not a criminal." Judge E. B. Belden insisted, "I am satisfied that what she did was done under the infatuation with and guilty influence of Kufahl," and added that she came from "very good family," some of whom he had known for years. Even Sheriff Wylie put in a plea for Myrtle.

A former neighbor of Myrtle's, Mrs. Fred N. Smith, was not so charitable. "I have nothing against her," Smith wrote, "but I know Mrs. Schaude is not safe to live with her children or anyone else." And Alfred Godfrey was incensed. "At the time of her trial and prior thereto, I understood that up until the time she murdered her husband she had led an exemplary life," he wrote. "I have positive proof in my possession now that such is not the case and it is my personal opinion that she should suffer the consequences of her act provided by the laws of this state." And a lawyer from Lake Geneva, Lewis G. Brown, wrote, "It appears to me senile for anyone to ever suggest parole for such a person where the sentence was so light. In my opinion, if this woman is entitled to parole, they should remove the locks on all of the doors in Waupun and apologize to every person there for having detained them at all."

Lawyers Seymour and Thorson argued mainly on two points: Myrtle's failing health and her children's need for her. They included a full report on Myrtle's physical condition from prison physician J. J. Bowes, M.D., who wrote that she was an "extreme neurotic," and that "her nerves are at a high tension which without restraint is liable to end in a complete nervous breakdown." He said that among other remedies, Myrtle had been given "Violet Ray" treatments without much effect. He also said she seemed to be aging very rapidly and called her a "model prisoner."

The lawyers also argued, "The Schaude people were people of intelligence and refinement. The children are exceptionally so... . They are at present without either a father's or mother's care and attention, the two oldest boys living with two separate families at Whitewater, Wisconsin, and there working their way through school; and the other two children with two sisters of Mrs. Schaude... ."

The governor wasn't buying it, however, and the plea was refused for the following reasons:

"Mrs. Schaude implicated another party, who was tried on a charge of murder and found not guilty by a jury. To what extent the other party had guilty knowledge I do not know. The theory in both cases was that these two parties desired to get rid of Mrs. Schaude's husband and the children so that they might marry and live a life without the impediment of children by a former marriage. Whatever offenses were committed or attempted, that seemed to be the motive. After it became known to Mrs. Schaude that her husband died from strychnine poisoning, which she had given him, whether purposely or negligently, she seemed to have had no remorse, as she gave to her children pieces of candy containing strychnine, knowing that death would result therefrom, thus carrying her designed motives into execution.

> *"The other party is free, and if Mrs. Schaude were released the original intent could be executed. She being an extreme neurotic, I cannot bring myself to the judgment that she is a safe person to be at liberty. Therefore denied."*
>
> —"J.J.B.," volume K, number 338, Wisconsin Pardon Dockets

In a nutshell, the judgment was that if freed, Myrtle could still get together with Kufahl, and that she was an "extreme neurotic" and therefore needed to be locked up. This decision did not prevent Myrtle from trying again in August of 1927 with a new governor, the same attorneys, and the same result. This time Myrtle wrote her own letter to Governor Fred R. Zimmerman, in her own handwriting.

"I am writing you in regard to my very own self," she wrote, "seems I can not write to you in a business form, but will have to write to you as a child would write to its father, begging you to forgive and have compassion for the wrong I have done, but why I did this wrong I do not know, *never* will I be able to read myself." She asked him for a chance to atone and "make up to those I have caused so much sorrow and suffering." "And believe me," she added, "when I say I have suffered, how I have suffered." She told him that she was "truly starving" for her children, and wanted to "take care of my little family, after I pick up and get rested from all of this." It was her highest desire to educate her four darling children, she continued, finishing with a promise. "In closing, I wish to tell you, that if ever I have any thing more to do with Ernst Kufahl I would ask to be put back in here for the rest of my life ..." and asked him to let her "show the world I can still be a woman and a good mother."

Somehow that must have failed to impress. But sticking to the old saying, "Three's the charm," Myrtle gave it another try in the beginning of January 1929, this time with Milwaukee attorney Herbert J. Piper arguing her case. The charm worked. Most of the same arguments were used, along with the facts that her hair had gone entirely gray and she had dropped from 118 pounds to 102. She was granted a conditional pardon and parole by Governor Fred R. Zimmerman barely five years after arriving at Waupun. Zimmerman was just leaving office, and, as is the custom for outgoing governors and presidents, he probably wrote a flurry of pardons days before Walter Kohler took over as governor.

Of course, Myrtle still had to report to a state parole office once a month, but she was out! She was released to a Methodist minister in Fond du Lac, Reverend Otis M. Johnson, said the *Whitewater Register* of January 10, 1929. Johnson was a former pastor and was one of those who wrote impassioned pleas for her pardon.

The *Whitewater Register* editor had visited Myrtle just a year and a half before her release and now expressed shock at her appearance. He wrote, "Mrs. Schaude, though but 42 years of age, has the appearance of a woman of 60. She is thin and frail and somewhat stooped. The prison experience broke her spirit though she received the kindliest treatment from those connected with the Institution."

The *Register* also noted that many people in Whitewater were not very happy about Myrtle's fast escape from behind bars.

> *"It is safe to say that the action of Governor Zimmerman in releasing Mrs. Schaude is generally condemned here. The diabolical plan to snuff out the life of her three* [sic] *children although they were saved by an eleventh hour repentance is unforgivable. So far as Mrs. Schaude is concerned her broken health and spirit insures society against future crime but whether or not her punishment has been sufficiently severe to deter other women with a sex complex from doing away with an unwanted husband is another matter. A majority of White-*

*water people hold to the opinion that the punishment was altogether insufficient for that purpose."*

—Whitewater Register, January 10, 1929

Myrtle's release from parole became final and official three years later, in 1932, and Myrtle was then completely free to go her own way "by her lonesome," as she once phrased it in a letter to Ernst Kufahl.

# Chapter Thirteen

## You Only Go Around Twice

Getting out of prison was one thing. Starting a new life where she wouldn't be quickly recognized as the "Poison Widow" was quite another. But despite her "frail and thin" condition upon release, Myrtle was up to life's challenges as usual.

Charles McGarrahan, second husband of Myrtle Schaude.—*Courtesy of McGarrahan family*

Evidence of exactly where she went from Fond du Lac after being released to the Reverend Otis Johnson is a bit sketchy, but various family sources have said she worked as a domestic in Oshkosh, ran a boardinghouse in Milwaukee, and traveled to Nebraska. She and Edward did own property there, so it's likely she would have gone to see and possibly sell it. It appears she was looking for male companionship, too.

A few years after her final clearance from the "big house," Myrtle placed a "lonely hearts" ad in an unknown newspaper, and it was answered by wid-

Myrtle Coad Schaude McGarrahan, in Zion, Illinois.
—*Courtesy of the McGarrahan family*

ower Charles McGarrahan, originally of Zion, Illinois. Charles wrote his sixteen-year-old daughter, Ruth, that he had met a woman by answering such an ad and was going to marry her. He did so in 1935 and eventually brought Myrtle back to Zion to meet his family.

It's hard to say whether Myrtle told her new husband about her criminal record and incarceration, or about how her first husband died, but certainly all of the other McGarrahans were blissfully ignorant of Myrtle's true past.

Myrtle's oldest two children, of course, were grown or close to it by the time she got out of prison. Even little Lawrence would have been eleven or twelve. The children seemed to do well where they were placed, building new lives for themselves. All but Delbert, who owned and operated a barbershop in Lake Geneva, Wisconsin, moved out of state. Delbert married Lulu Baumbach in 1941. They never had children, but two of Lulu's nieces remember "Uncle Del" as a "great person." They were vaguely aware that Del's mother had given him poison candy, but it was something no one in the family liked to talk about, they said.

Ralph, nicknamed Buck, was a teacher and supervisor of industrial arts at Southeast High School in Wichita, Kansas. He died in 1979 and was not survived by children, according to his obituary. Mae seemed to have stayed the closest to Myrtle. The McGarrahan family remembered more visits from Mae than from her brothers, and Myrtle moved near Mae to spend her last days. The three older children had died by the time this book went to press, but Lawrence was still living in another state at the time. (Myrtle's surviving descendants who were contacted elected not to comment for this book.)

It appears that all of the children had always kept quiet about what their mother had done, at least where her "new" family was concerned. It is understandable that they would not have wanted to start the publicity up again, or upset the McGarrahans. They evidently trusted that Myrtle was through with strychnine for good. There seems to be no compelling reason to think otherwise.

Myrtle's stepgranddaughter, Kathlyn Gay, is a much-published nonfiction author now living in Florida. She remembers Myrtle well, as do her three brothers and her sons. She and other family members recall Myrtle often saying that Charles was an easy man to get along with. As far as anyone remembers, the couple had no marital problems.

Myrtle's second marriage lasted seventeen years—eerily, the same as her first. Charles McGarrahan sold electrical appliances when they were first married but was working as a drapery salesman for his brother Don's company (while Myrtle sewed the draperies) when Charles fell ill. He died May 11, 1952, at Highwood Hospital of a cerebral hemorrhage, according to the death certificate. There was no autopsy. He had been in the hospital for two months and was sick for two previous months at home. He didn't seek medical attention at first because, like many people in Zion, he was of a religious mind-set that preferred to try healing by faith and prayer first. Charles was a member of First Baptist Church in Waukegan, but family members recall that he and Myrtle attended a Methodist church in Zion during their marriage.

Kathlyn's brother Jim McGarrahan was in high school at the time of his grandfather's death and believes that Charles had a stroke before entering the hospital. At any rate, Charles was incapacitated enough while still at home that Myrtle had to call on Kathlyn's father, Kenneth

McGarrahan, to come over and help get her husband in and out of the bathtub.

After Charles died, Myrtle worked in a Chicago suburb as a maid and then was hired by Kenneth and his wife, Beatrice, as a housekeeper so that Myrtle would have sufficient work history to get Social Security income. Myrtle's help at home was undoubtedly welcome because Kenneth worked as a full-time accountant for Zion Industries for awhile and he and Beatrice also established a laundry and dry-cleaning business.

By the time her parents hired Myrtle, Kathlyn Gay had already married and moved out of their home on Ezekiel Avenue, but her youngest brothers were still there, and Kathlyn often visited with her husband and children.

"When our two boys visited their grandparents, they never liked Myrtle," said Kathlyn. "They often recall a time when they were supposed to be sleeping in an upstairs bedroom next to Myrtle's room (my old bedroom) and the two boys were bouncing around on the beds like kids do, and Myrtle came in with her hair up in curlers to scold. The boys thought they'd seen a witch, they said."

Myrtle seemed to have a strong desire to be praised for her cooking skills, the family noted. Kathlyn's brother Jim, one of those who still lived at home while Myrtle was there, said she always wanted approval on her meals. "I particularly remember the apple pie ... wanting to know if it was as good as what mother made," he said. "I would not give her complete satisfaction. It was almost as good, but not quite."

Kathlyn Gay's son, Douglas Gay, also remembered Myrtle "fishing for compliments" on her food. "In fact, if there's any comment I would associate with her," he said, "it would be, 'Isn't that good?' in reference to her cooking. Looking back, maybe it was her 'triumph' that everyone was able to leave the table alive." Douglas added that he didn't have many memories, good or bad, associated with Myrtle. "It was just a relationship in name only with no substance to it."

Douglas also said he always felt uneasy around Myrtle. "I recall that as a kid I never felt comfortable when she was around me," he said, "whether alone or with other people in the room. I don't know if you would call that my 'kid radar' kicking in or what, but I could never feel any sense of peace when she was in the room. Obviously, no one knew about her past, and even if it was known, I find it hard to believe anyone would have exposed a minor to that kind of information."

Another of Kenneth McGarrahan's sons, John Richard, also lived at home when Myrtle was housekeeper, and he said, "while others thought of her as mean, I only recall her as somewhat stern." It seems Myrtle used to insist John Richard wash all the windows in the house once a week, a chore not all the family members agreed needed to be done so often.

Jim McGarrahan does remember Myrtle as spirited and energetic. "I remember her complaining about her age at age seventy. She would go out with others her age and not like being with that age person or not wanting to be that old," he said. He also remembers Myrtle's daughter Mae coming to visit with her husband and daughter, who was about his age, and making trips to Wisconsin to visit Myrtle's son Delbert. Evidently Myrtle recovered completely, at least physically, from her five years in prison.

Charles McGarrahan's sons, including Kenneth, all died relatively young from apparently heart-related problems. Kathlyn Gay noted, "My father had diabetes and his death could have been attributed to that."

Another of Kathlyn's brothers, "Charlie" McGarrahan, noted that their father, Kenneth, died of "a coronary arrest," although he'd had an EKG three months earlier that had not shown any problems with his heart. The doctors decided his diabetes must have "masked" the heart problem, said Charlie.

Myrtle eventually went to live in a nursing home near her daughter Mae, survived to the ripe, old age of eighty-eight, and died December 16, 1974. She was buried next to her husband, Charles, in Mount Olivet Cemetery in Zion, far from her own family graveyard in Siloam, Wisconsin.

So, did "the Poison Widow" truly redeem and reform herself? Although concealing one's past and reforming it are not exactly the same thing, Myrtle buried her personal history well enough that her second family never suspected a thing until this writer arrived one day with old newspaper clippings in hand. Learning of Myrtle's former life was a shock to them, and yet, according to

Kathlyn Gay, there had always been a somewhat chilly reserve around Myrtle. "She used to spend her time doing needlepoint," remembered Kathlyn, "and we had a chair with a cushion that was covered with one of her needlepoint pieces. We always called it Myrtle's chair. When my mother died and the household was sold, no one wanted to take it." The chair was eventually sold to someone outside the family.

Myrtle did seem to cling to religion in her later years. After Charles died, Myrtle joined the Christian Catholic Church (no relation to the Roman Catholic Church) in Zion, an institution that had been founded by a zealous Australian preacher named John Alexander Dowie. Dowie built the city of Zion around the turn of the nineteenth century as his idea of a new "paradise on earth." He became famous for an attack he wrote on his "enemies" in Chicago titled "Zion's Holy War Against the Hosts of Hell in Chicago" and held to a literal interpretation of the Bible. Although Dowie was no longer in charge by the time Myrtle joined, she evidently felt at home with Dowie's philosophies. And she remained a faithful churchgoer, just as she had been in Palmyra and Whitewater. No one, of course, can say what her true beliefs and motivations were regarding her church attendance in Zion.

Ernst Kufahl also managed to live a quiet life. He never did get his farm in Minnesota. He moved to nearby Fort Atkinson, where he worked at the Jamesway Factory, manufacturing cow stanchions and taking solitary bachelor meals at the Blackhawk Hotel, according to Ed Messerschmidt of rural Elkhorn, Wisconsin.

Messerschmidt worked with Kufahl at Jamesway in 1947 and 1948 and then became a relative-by-marriage of Kufahl's when Kufahl married Messerschmidt's aunt, Frances Beahlen, on July 3, 1952. Frances already had several children from a previous marriage and was seven years older than Kufahl (Myrtle had been eight years his senior). Messerschmidt described his aunt as a "friendly, good-natured person" and noted that because she lived only a few blocks from the Blackhawk Hotel, it's possible that's where she and Kufahl met. Strangely, the year of Kufahl's marriage was the same year Myrtle's second husband died, and his wedding took place not quite two months after Charles McGarrahan's death.

Headstone of Myrtle McGarrahan's grave, Mt. Olivet Cemetery, Zion, Illinois.
—*Linda Godfrey*

Is it possible that Kufahl and Myrtle secretly kept in touch and that, as he had done years earlier while living in Minnesota, he taunted Myrtle by mail with news of his sweetheart and impending marriage? Was she hoping she could still have him if only she were free again? That's pure speculation, of course, because no evidence exists that they had a relationship of any sort over the years, and it is probably only an ironic coincidence that Kufahl ended his bachelorhood with someone else just about the time it would have been possible for him to finally be with Myrtle.

Still, it's not hard to imagine that two people who once were in love and wrote each other every single day, sometimes twice a day, for a year might somehow have been tempted to correspond again—especially because Kufahl stayed single for so long. And while Myrtle was careful to stick to her second-round role as hard-working wife and family cook, Kufahl's personality still seemed that of the "oddest duck" as he approached middle age. Because Fort Atkinson is only about a ten-minute drive from Whitewater, it's likely his reputation preceded him in that town. And that probably didn't help his eligibility in the eyes of most women.

"He was always kind of half-laughing," said Ed Messerschmidt. "There were a couple of older fellows that poked fun at him and told stories." Still, Kufahl's late-life bride often told family members that "Ernie" always treated her very well.

Kufahl had one other unwanted brush with fame in regard to the "Poison Widow" trials. In 1937, the *Whitewater Register* reported that Ernst Kufahl was suing an unnamed detective magazine for libel for telling the story of the Poison Widow and implicating Kufahl in the murder plot. Unfortunately, the paper did not say which publication it was that he sued or how the suit came out. It can be said that Kufahl did not appear to get suddenly rich. Kufahl did nothing else after that to draw media attention for the rest of his life, and he died leaving no known offspring of his own.

It is remarkable just how quietly the sensational "Poison Widow" story finally played itself out, given the shocking events in the saga. Both Myrtle Schaude and Ernst Kufahl, outwardly the most ordinary of human beings, evidently possessed some inner quirk that had once enabled them to step outside their societal and religious boundaries. But when all the shouting was over, they were each able to fade back into the community woodwork.

It's interesting to consider what might have happened if Myrtle had been successful in her plan to kill her children by poison and car crash. Because it appeared so hard for anyone to ever believe she was capable of

Myrtle Schaude's Whitewater home as it appears today —*Linda Godfrey*

murder, she might well have escaped suspicion a second time and lived happily ever after with Ernst as his "fussy little fairy."

But could they really have lived happily, knowing what the price had been? At the very least, it's a safe bet they would each have been keeping one eye sharply on the rat poison, with prune juice banned forever from the menu.

It's a pity Edward Schaude couldn't have done as much.

# Postscript

by Dr. Adam F. Wooten, D.O.

## Could Myrtle Schaude Have Successfully Used an Insanity Defense if She Were on Trial Today?

The reporter for the *Elkhorn Independent* newspaper in Wisconsin called it "a drama that has attracted nation-wide interest" when describing the case of a woman who had attempted to kill her four children. If reading that phrase today, it would be difficult to know which case he was referring to. There have been several recent cases of national interest concerning women who had killed their children, such as those of Susan Smith and Andrea Yates.

Due to the media attention cases like these attract, the public has become more aware of mothers who kill or attempt to kill their children, but this behavior is not a new phenomenon. In fact, it is an issue that society has been dealing with for hundreds of years. The aforementioned quote from the *Elkhorn Independent* was not made recently. It was printed in February 1924 and was related to the case of Myrtle Schaude, "the Poison Widow."

Are all mothers who kill or attempt to kill their children "evil" or "monsters"? No. There are many complex motives and behaviors that lead a mother to attempt to do what society perceives as the unthinkable: purposely harming your own children.

Andrea Yates drowned her five children in June 2001. Mental health experts for both the prosecution and the defense examined Mrs. Yates. All concluded that she was psychotic at the time she killed her children and was acting in what she perceived was the children's best interest, but she was still unsuccessful raising an insanity defense.

Susan Smith killed her two children in October 1994. Even though she did not raise an insanity defense, her attorney—in an attempt to mitigate her penalty—included that she suffered from emotional difficulties. Some concluded that Susan Smith was depressed and suicidal at the time she killed her children, but a large percentage of the public thought her motive was to improve her desirability in the eyes of a man with whom she was having an affair. Some readers may view the case of Myrtle Schaude as closely resembling that of Susan Smith.

Mrs. Schaude attempted to kill her four children, ages sixteen, thirteen, nine, and five, by poisoning them with strychnine in September 1923. If her actions had been committed today, her defense attorney might have attempted to prove she was legally insane at the time of the crime. The current Wisconsin insanity statute states: "A person is not responsible for criminal conduct if at the time of such conduct as result of mental disease or defect the person lacked substantial capacity to either appreciate the wrongfulness of his or her conduct or conform his or her conduct to the requirements of the law."

Could Myrtle Schaude have successfully used an insanity defense? Based on the limited information available, a psychiatrist would not be capable to offer an opinion, with reasonable medical certainty, on Mrs. Schaude's motives or state of mind on September 21, 1923. However, after reading *The Poison Widow*, I found it interesting to analyze the case and hypothesize what could have motivated her actions.

Dr. Phillip Resnick, M.D., a forensic psychiatrist, is the nation's leading expert on cases involving child murder by parents. He authored the classic article "Child Murder by Parents: A Psychiatric Review of Filicide" in 1969 and has continued to research the subject since. *Filicide* is the term used when a parent kills a child older than twenty-four hours, and the term *neonaticide* is used when the victim is a newborn. Filicide and neonaticide are two completely different phenomenons with different behavioral aspects and motives. Head trauma, strangulation, and drowning are the most common methods of both filicide and neonaticide. Poisoning represents only approximately 6 percent of the methods used by mothers to kill their children. Child victims are at the greatest risk within their first year of life. The percentage of filicide victims who fall within five to eighteen years of age total only 21 percent.

Dr. Resnick has further classified filicides into one of five apparent motives: altruistic, acutely psychotic, unwanted child, fatal maltreatment, and spouse revenge. Although this system of categorization was developed more than thirty years ago, it remains the standard in classifying motives of parents who kill their children.

In altruistic filicides a mother is often depressed and thinking of committing suicide. She cannot imagine her children living without a mother and takes their lives believing it is in their best interest. This is the most common motive of mothers who kill their children. However, in many cases the mothers do not go on to commit suicide afterward. There is often a feeling of relief from believing they have done "the right thing." In some cases, the sense of relief ends immediate thoughts of suicide. These mothers usually make no attempt to conceal their crime.

An acutely psychotic filicide involves a mother who takes actions as a result of psychosis, such as hearing voices or having unusual or bizarre beliefs due to a mental illness. An illness such as schizophrenia is a common etiology. For example, Andrea Yates had both altruistic and psychotic motives. She believed, due to psychosis, that if she did not kill her children while they were innocent, they would suffer an eternity in hell.

Perhaps the most disturbing motives are those of unwanted child, fatal maltreatment, or spousal revenge. An unwanted child filicide is simply a homicide committed because the child is no longer desired or wanted by the parent. A mental illness is not always present in the cases of an unwanted child.

Fatal maltreatment is child abuse or "battered child syndrome" that results in death. Research has indicated this is the most common cause of child homicide in the United States.

Spousal revenge filicide occurs when the motive is to make the other parent suffer. An example could include a mother who discovers that her husband is having an affair or ready to leave her and she deliberately kills their children in an attempt to make her husband suffer or "get back at him."

Based on the media coverage of recent child-murder-by-parent cases, one could think this is a progressively growing problem. However, the reported rate of child murder by parent in children less than one year of age has remained relatively stable over the past twenty years. It is also difficult to imagine that one would not always be suffering from a major mental illness in order to commit such acts. In reality however, approximately 7 percent of parents who kill their children have no psychiatric diagnosis at all, and approximately 12 percent suffer from disorders of character.

Psychiatrists refer to disorders of character as personality disorders. A personality disorder is a fixed lifelong pattern of behavior that interferes with one's functioning. One example is that of a narcissistic personality disorder, in which a person has an inflated sense of self-importance and special entitlement and often lacks empathy for others. Another example perhaps to consider in the case of Myrtle Schaude is that of a dependent personality disorder, in which a person tends to allow other people to make decisions and assume responsibility for him or her because of poor self-confidence. A personality disorder is not generally considered a severe mental disease or defect for the purpose of an insanity defense.

When a forensic psychiatrist examines a defendant to determine his or her "sanity at the time of the act," the psychiatrist is interested in behaviors immediately before, during, and after an act. Insanity criteria vary from state to state, but most include the key concept of "knowledge of wrongfulness at the time of the act." Behaviors that occur before and after an act are important to an examining forensic psychiatrist for a number of reasons. For example, behaviors such as making efforts to avoid detection, dispose of evidence, and avoid apprehension before and after a crime indicate that a defendant did have knowledge of the wrongfulness of his or her actions.

Would Myrtle Schaude have met the legal standard for insanity today? First, was she suffering from a mental illness on September 21, 1923? She had previously had a "nervous breakdown" in 1912 and went into a "hysterical state" in the county jail shortly after confessing to her crime. But just prior to the poisonings, she was running a boarding club for girls and successfully managing between twenty-six and thirty boarders on her own. She also had planned the poisonings at least one week ahead of the crime and made arrangements for the children to drive a neighbor's vehicle after the poisonings, both of which indicate an organized thought process. Is there any evidence to suggest she was having a severe emotional disturbance at the time she gave her children strychnine-laced candy?

Second, even if she was suffering from a mental illness on September 21, 1923, did it cause her to not know the wrongfulness of her actions? In her confession on September 22, 1923, she clearly stated that she gave her children pieces of candy that she had put strychnine in. She further stated she knew the strychnine was poison and that it would kill the children. She was not specifically asked, "Did you know it was wrong to attempt to kill your children?" but some of her actions indicated that she did have knowledge of the wrongfulness of her actions. For example, prior to her confession she had fabricated a story of another woman passing out poisoned candy in an apparent attempt to conceal her involvement.

What motivated Mrs. Schaude to attempt to murder her children? That is a complex question, especially if considering one of five possible motives. Mrs. Schaude had made no comments before, during, or after her crime to suggest she believed the children would be better off if they were dead. As mentioned previously, there does not appear to be any evidence she was psychotic at the time of her crime.

She had no history of physically abusing her children, and because they were not actually killed, fatal maltreatment is eliminated. Spousal revenge was not a possibility because her husband was no longer alive, and the reason behind that is an entirely different and interesting discussion.

Out of Dr. Resnick's five classifications of apparent motives of mothers who murder their children, that leaves an unwanted child as the final behavioral motive to consider. Did Myrtle Schaude have something so important to her that would make a once-loving mother no longer want her children and attempt to kill them? I have formed my opinion, and I will allow the readers of this incredible story to form theirs.

**About Dr. Adam F. Wooten, D.O., Forensic Psychiatrist:**

Dr. Adam F. Wooten, D.O., received his bachelor of science degree in 1991 from Marshall University in Huntington, West Virginia, and his doctor of osteopathy in 1997 from the West Virginia School of Osteopathic Medicine in Lewisburg, West Virginia. He completed four years of residency training in psychiatry at the University of Kentucky, six months as a congressional fellow on Capitol Hill working for Senator Arlen Specter, and one year of specialty training in psychiatry and the law. His forensic psychiatry fellowship was at Case Western Reserve University under the direction of Phillip J. Resnick, M.D. Wooten has published a number of professional articles and papers, such as "The Safety and Role of Clinicians Treating Violent Offenders," *Resident Reporter*, August 2000 and "The Andrea Yates Case: Lessons for Forensic Fellows." *American Academy of Psychiatry and the Law Newsletter*, 2002. He has won awards such as Outstanding Resident Teacher from the University of Kentucky Department of Psychiatry and the C. Everett Koop Resident Physician Leader from Dartmouth. He also had the opportunity to contribute to the nationally known case *State of Texas v. Andrea Yates*. Dr. Wooten currently resides in Cincinnati, Ohio.

# Appendix

## The Letters of Myrtle Schaude and Ernst Kufahl Preserved as State's Evidence

December 10, 1922, Whitewater, Wisconsin

Dear Ernst, Sunday afternoon—

Dinner over and work all done went to church this morning and I read paper and some in a story book Ralph has from the library, and I guess this day will never pass. The girls up stairs are having a good time have two other girls up there. This is a lovely day for a winters day, am wondering what you are doing this afternoon. Next Sunday afternoon we will be close by each other. Grace wants to go to the Museum next Sunday afternoon, and to a Catholic Church in the fore noon, and we will go to some other church. I think she is going to stay with some one on third street or she thinks she will, if she does not stay there she will go to some other people. I wish you were here with me this afternoon, the children are out playing or rather up to the Normal with Esther and Gifford Loomer on the swings, and the boys are over to Tafts, and I am here all by my lonely.

Evelyn Heire left Friday nite, just think she said she wanted me to pay her room rent. I let her talk for a while then I told her she better go some where else, so Friday nite she left, and it surely has helped all the rest since she left. They sure are very much different, better in every way. It was quite cold here yesterday morning, 3 above and this morning it was quite cold, but I have it nice and warm in here, had the dining room up to 70 by breakfast time this morning, am burning the siftings to day, if I keep the draft open they burn good and give a lot of heat.

Stunt nite was very good, was disappointed you did not come. Think you would of enjoyed it. I am going to the Dentist again.

Have you heard any more about what they are going to do with you, maybe they will keep you there, only change your course. Will send you some more eats to morrow afternoon or Tuesday, I wish they would keep it warmer for you, it is so easy to catch cold sitting in a cool room, take good care of your self and do not work to hard.

Jennie and Merritt did not come, thought it to cold to bring the baby, she telephoned yesterday and said they would come some other time. Had a good sermon this morning.

The drain from the bath seemed to be filled up again, so had the plumber come up, it was all running back in the cellar where that that basin is in the laundry well they fussed around here and found nothing the matter with the pipes in the house so then they dug a hole out in front and found out the main sewer on the street was filled up and it was all backing up in here, such a mess, they had to dig the hole out of lawn, well when they got done the plumber gave me a bill of $14. I thought over it once or twice and I thought seeing the trouble was not in our pipes or drain that I had no business paying for the city sewer and I <u>told him so</u>, well he said I was the one that called him up and I was the one to pay, but still I did not feel right about it, so called up Mr. Sprackling and told him how things stood, and he said the city would have to pay for all that. I feel better now about it, so you see any one has to be on the look out all the time, maybe Mr. Horne thought he could get pay out of me and the city, too, but if he did he got fooled. Mr. Sprackling told me he was glad I had more brains and sense than some women. Ha Ha. Some would of paid on the spur of the moment <u>I nearly did</u> but did not you see.

I wish I was done with the Dentist, he told me I had one of the smallest mouths he ever worked in, it doesn't look so from the outside, does it. Ha Ha.

I washed your yellow shirt yesterday, and I will mend it as good as I can, and if you need it I will send it or bring it Saturday. I guess Grace is going to do some shopping in the ore noon. I may do a little but not very much that I know about now.

Vacation will be here soon. I am always glad to have them come, ain't you? If I had that book here this afternoon I could do some reading...

... do not know I am sure why I did not sleep, seemed to be tired, too, and then when I did go to sleep I had the dearest little dream about you, will tell you when I see you if I do not forget.

Going to get up early and wash to morrow just got the machine back the other day you took down when you were here. Sakes alive I know you must be tired reading such a letter so will close and let you rest. Guess I could write on for ever.

Mr. Helbing is not feeling quite so well, guess the ride home was too much for him, the girls say he looks very bad. Now I am going to slice the potatoes for supper.

Sincerely, your little girlie... write to me to nite!

December 12, 1922, Milwaukee County School of Agriculture, Wauwatosa, Wisconsin

Dear Myrtle,

It is too cold for to take a pleasure trip that's why I stayed home this evening. Last night I was to several Packing Houses to get some Sheep Tallow for to send home to Mother. At one of the Packing Houses, they told me that they would butcher sheep to-day and save the tallow for me. But it is so cold today. Max Nemitz will go there tomorrow, provided the weather is warmer. He has no alcohol in his radiator and is not going to risk freezing it. You know they do freeze easy in weather like this. Is'pose you don't use your car lately. They are really too much bother unless you have a good car and garage. A good radiator with alcohol and a warm garage. Do you know that it would be foolish for you to buy an open car. Just think about 6 months cold weather. Those people with the closed cars looked so comfortable last Sunday but it seemed cold in a car with curtains all around. A coupe or a sedan are the only cars where a person can enjoy automobiling. I have not heard anything concerning my training lately. Mr. Wright sees me often but does not mention anything to me. I think he decided to let me alone. Why do you always ask me whether I think you done right. Does your conscience bother you when you tell people the truth. I think that it just showed that you know how to be and are able to run a business. You could work for others all the time if you would not stick for your rights. Try it once and you would soon see that you would be ruled by everybody. You are doing good, but if the furnace makes so much work then why don't you let the two boys tend to it? Those two boys ought to be able to do that much for you if they think anything of their mother. You can afford to pay Ralph and Delbert a small amount every week and then they would be glad to do it… .

I would always sooner tell the people just what I think of them but they don't always care to hear the truth… .

So this will be the last letter, but I will send the laundry if I don't forget it, tomorrow. Don't plan on having me loaf around your place all vacation, because I am not. I am going to spend some time at home and with the company, if they do come.

So you are going to church more lately. You see it can be done if people want to go. Did you get lonesome Sunday… . You ought to have a steady coming and take you out for a ride once in a while, etc. I'spose Mr. Jordan is boarding at your place now maybe he would enjoy tending to the furnace. And he is not so y … o … u … n … g either is he. I am glad that I was not there when you wrote that letter or I might have gotten a wet hand. My hands chap lately. What is good for chapped hands. It is nice and warm in our room lately. We always have the window open nights.

I just read over your letter again and I think that the company or city ought to pay you for damages done by that sewer in your basement. Tell them so next time. Ha ha. Your mouth may be small but oh my big enough for many purposes. Is it smaller than what it looks to be from the outside. I'spose it is hard to work in. Maybe he likes to get the whole hand in it. You can let that shirt there. I may buy me a new one this week. I looked at something fuzzy last nite but oh my too much for me at present. But I know it looks just beautiful. Well I am slow lately with eating the eats. I drink too much lately. Just paid my milk bill from Wed. To tomorrow 42 cents but I get a qt. for 6 cents every once in a while. Good by.

Sincerely, Ernst.

Date unknown, Whitewater, Wisconsin,
State Exhibit C, read into trial records of Ernst Kufahl

Dear Ernst,

Well now that is quite a joke. Since I read this nice little letter I remember you did say something about extra charges, but honestly at the time I did not even more than just notice what you said. And another joke: I didn't put any cream in that glass of milk. I poured it in the glass at supper time, and I guess the cream must have come to the top, and you see you got the cream first at that time. And as for the fifty cents, Ernst, I will take it this time, seeing you want me to, but really those few handkerchiefs I washed, I like to do it, just love to wash them for you; and every week if you have any you want washed let me do it. Please don't think you have to pay me extra because I don't want anything. By being so good to me as you are, that more than pays for all I do for you. I know your little tongue is in a wet place, but it never slips too much. Mine is also. As for being good, you are good enough, and careful. You know the old saying if you can't be good be careful. So I guess that is what we will have to do. Now, dear Ernst, don't think you have to look at every word before you speak, because you don't. Now, I am wondering why you can't understand me. Well, Ernst, that must be the nature of the beast. I have been told that by many all my life. My goodness, such a long letter. I could write a lot more. Isn't it funny I can write to some people better than others. I wonder why. Ernst, I was told once awhile ago that I was too honest in my saying, wording, looks and feelings; but so it goes. I can't help that either. But I can always be careful.

Sincerely, Your Little Milk Maid.

July 8, 1923, McGrath, Minnesota

Dear Myrtle,

Sunday P.M. and it is real warm but nice and breezy here today. I wanted to write with the machine but some strap busted on it and I don't care to fix it "Leave it to Warren" it is his machine. Your both letters from July 1 and 3rd. were received and I am always glad to get them. I was working a few hrs. the 4th and did not go to the village. We had a heavy rain shower here in the afternoon so I did not work much. I had Arnold Gunufson hired for blasting Thursday. We also rode to a farmer who had lumber for sale and I bought $14.25 worth of two by fours for a garage. Friday I cut some more trees and brush and in the evening I hired Hansen to take me and Mr. Schoenrock to a sawmill where Mr. Schoenrock had 2500 of pine lumber for sale. He wanted $33.00 per thousand ft. I bought the whole lot, which will cost me about $4.00 and $5.00 per thousand for to get it planed, etc. It will cost about $38.00 delivered. A person needs an ice box here too, but I have nothing yet. Thank you for the recipe, but I don't like the way this bach keeps the grease and that's why I will not make any until I have a place where I can do my own cooking all my way. No I am not gaining so that I notice it. The eats do not always suit and the water here I only drink boiled. Oranges are 65 cents pr. doz. here. I used to buy them for 50 cents pr. doz. For dinner we had boiled potatoes, boiled eggs, fried summer sausage, lemonade, wheat and rye bread peanut and other butter. The desert was all gone which we had sent to us from Whitewater. We also had prunes and apricots cooked together but I did not eat any, they look all right tho. Are you bothered much with flies? I swated one here to-day and a few more are bothering me now. Yesterday I had a man and team hired to haul poplar trees on a pile from where I am planning to build. We hauled 16 loads from about 2 1/2 acres. The loads were not big but I think that I will have about 100 loads which is cut now but will have to be hauled together later after I can get a team and time to do it. Everything is all right.

Sincerely Yours, Ernst. H. W. K.

# Appendix

August 19, 1923, McGrath, Minnesota

Dear Myrtle,

Your four cards were rec'd. Three Friday evening. Mr. Gunnufson had taken the mail to his place then McNary took it further and when I went after it Bundy had it. You folks made very good time. I did not get home until Thursday noon and you were at Watertown Thursday nite already. Thursday P.M. after I made dinner etc. I oiled the private office. Friday I oiled the West South and about 2/3 of the East side of the garage. Then I was all out of oil. Yesterday morning we had a heavy Thunder rain at 1 P.M. and it leaked on the pillow, so I got up and held a aluminum cup there until the rain was over about 1:20 P.M. I took the latter and looked why it leaked but could not find any place where there was a hole or shingles layed wrong. I must tell you something but keep it for yourself. The damp weather and I got chilled, I think was the cause of it, anyhow I dreamed that I had to p and I could just see myself and really it happened a bit but I soon woke. That's the first time in years I think. The dream is what done it. It was not much a spot as big as my hand. I hung the sheet and feather bed on the line. I don't think it damaged the feathers any. But such is luck, and then I waited for Gimpel to give me the figure of the lumber needed, but he had given them to the other carpenter and did not stop in the morning at my place. I had Crouch's team ordered but had to walk way to McNary's barn almost to the pine tree near the hall for the figures, and then when I called up the Lbr. Yd. They did not have it. Then I walked to Crouch's to get a pail of water and let them know that I did not need the team when Bundy and Werst rode by and I rode to town with them to get some groceries. I got some fresh pork 2 lbs. for 10 cents a lb. We were back at 12 n. I then fried the meat and made dinner. Washed clothes as I did not have a permit to burn brush and it was rather windy too. Then I took a bath using the washtub tho, because it is less bother to empty it. I made supper and changed clothes. I felt so lonesome that I walked to the Dance. I stayed until it nearly was over 2 P.M. this morning. That was really their first dance and I too helped pay, but did not dance. Dahlgren and Cressman done so too. They made o.k. but had much ice cream left which they wanted to sell to the men in the colony. I stayed in bed until 7:30 this morning. After breakfast I walked to Gunnufson's and brought back a jar. I got some milk Friday nite and told him to save me some every day whenever they think of going by here. I had some of that milk this morning which was thick and I wanted to make pancakes but they stuck to the pan and were no good. So I had toast. What do you s'pose was the matter. I s'pose the milk was too sour according to Mrs. Gunnufson's talk. I have been a real baby since you left. The day when I came back to McGrath my hands just shook. I wrote a letter to the folks in the Bank waiting for some one from here come in so I could ride out. I have felt terrible blue ever since I got back. Often I would sing to myself "I need thee every hour." This morning West gave me a good hint. He said that he would feel blue too if he would keep on brooding the lonesomeness and then he said that song may mean the woman had to do the leading. That's the trouble with me too. I get discourage and sometimes feel like running away. I was thinking of you what you have gone through etc. and always took it good natured. But I think that I need you worse than ever now. Really you don't know how I have felt about being so far away from you the last few days. I want you to tell me something when you answer this letter. Do you think I made a mistake for going up here? Do you honestly like it here, and think we could live happy and contented? Plumb's mother in law was here lately and now his wife is gone to Wisconsin with her mother. He is baching it now and said that maybe his wife would not come back. You see there one thinks different than the other. If I really knew that we would live happy here and make go then I would feel more contented. Everything seems to cost quite much anyhow the building and clearing. I do think it is better to get it all under cultivation now that I started at it, then to leave it the way it is. They have 2 ten ton tractors and one five ton here in Silver Star now. I ought to feel all right, but I have too much of a longing for some one now. I never wanted to let on but this time I just can not keep it for myself. I will have to brace up and think and do more work hereafter, then I'spose it will go better. This cooking for one etc. is nothing for me.

Jack Crouch wanted to buy Del's fish pole and I once promised him that I would let him have it, but don't think it's right you can ask Delbert whether he wants it or not. He has line sinker and hook on it. I wanted to store it inside the other day but it is too long. I will write to the folks. How are the children all? I s'pose Lawrence was glad to see you back home. So would I, but in different conditions. I am glad that you have thought of me and sent those cards. I s'pose I will receive your letter tomorrow. I wish that I was with you now fore ever. You are the only one that will ever make a man out of me. I will take your advise at all times.

Sincerely yours, Ernst Kufahl.

(Post Script) Monday morning 6:30 A.M. Had to put on my sweater being so cold in this garage. I found that dish which Del had in a box under the bed. Be it ever so humble there is no place like with me.

August 22, 1923, McGrath, Minnesota

Dear Myrtle,

Your letter was rec'd today and I sat down on the road grader and read all my mail. I almost missed the mail man but I yeld at him and he waited and took a letter along for some jane in Whitewater. I had quite a bit mail, a letter from home, a card from F. Bretschneider and, a letter from F. Braun asking me to write etc. The old sweet heart of mine still thot of me Sunday when I was lonesome here. That's the girl to whom I was half engaged. She asked me to wait a year or two and now she is that old, 21 years past since May 2. What shall I write to her. I am going to tell her that she is too late now that I am engaged to a woman with four children. Or what would you write to her? What have you told Ralph Saturday at supper table? So you thought of me Saturday nite, well I thought of you nearly all the time since you left me. I think more of you now then ever before. I often sit and read your mail and think of you where I ought to be out working. Mr. Werst was here a few minutes yesterday A.M. I could be busy at all times but to-day I have not done much. I helped the carpenters lay the stone inside of the house to make the floor stronger and then picked up shavings and watched them quite much so I got it done the way I want it. This P.M. Korschgen and I rode to town to get window frames. Lime, brick, windows, doors, locks, etc. I will have to get laths, and plaster, second flooring and the woodwork for inside yet. It will be a quite expensive little bungalow after it is all done. I got one nifty lock for the front door which I can set so it opens from the inside by turning the knob but has to be opened with a key from the outside. The doors cost about 5.75 each. So you see I can always take time to do my own washing. After about six weeks or so I will have much more time than money. It takes money to send clothes, but time to wash them. I have more time so I will do my own washing. I wish that I had a car then I surely would had gone for a long ride Sunday but as it is I had to stay home. Maybe some day I can afford one and have a real standard of living too. I think that you would live much better and comfortable where you are than up north here. But I would like to have you right here. Ha Ha. I'spose you would have to be very near here in winter otherwise I could not spend the week end with you anyhow. Just stop and consider things before selling your place there. Here the snow gets quite deep some winters and I have no car nor horse to get to town. It would be quite a job to walk 6 1/2 miles and back, 13 miles every week in a cold blizzard. Oh. My! A house like you and I like would cost at least $4000. At 8% interest = $320.00 pr. Yr. $26.75 pr. month the interest on the building would be. The bachelors house will be just about done till plastering this week. Is'pose it will be about 2 weeks at least before I can move in there. It does not seem quite so cold to-night. Good bye. I burnt that box of waste paper and found 3 bunches of your hair. It's 9:30 now so will get ready for bed. I visited at Crouch's tonite. Her initials are J.S. Crouch Route 2. Next week I will get some work done on the field. I am getting lazy lately. I stay in bed late about 6:45 every morning. I have not rec'd the eats yet, I may get it to nite. I surely am thinking of you all the time. I guess I am plumb nuts over you, as Werst says he was over a jane. Good nite. Sincerely yours, Ernst. P.S. Save my mail or send it back whatever you want to. That is a nice card and also the letter shows that the kid is thinking of me sometimes. Mr. Werst just delivered the eats to me now. Thank you very much. Will go to town soon.

August 30, 1923, McGrath, Minnesota

Dear Myrtle,

Your both letters and the eats have abeen rec'd yesterday. Thank you very much for the eats. I was all out of bread when I got it too. I bought a loaf of bread from Mr. Crouch this eve. I am eating some of your cookies now. It is 9:15 P.M. Have written a letter to the folks at home. I have all the brush burnt now, and helped haul poplars this P.M. I have about near forty cords on piles now and expect about fifty to sixty more. Then I want to buy some hard wood for the heater, so I can keep a fire all nite and day with out much bother. It would be quite a job to keep comfortable with green poplars this winter. We did not have rain here Monday, it looked as tho it might rain in the morning but later it was a swell day. I have the plaster and sand ready but not plastered yet. Maybe he will come to-morrow or Saturday to do the plastering. You wrote that you wished you could be nearer, 10 miles or a thousand is almost the same here. I have no way of getting anywheres. Mr. Schoenrock who is working for me now and maybe until November is going to let me have his buggy horse and buggy free of charge tomorrow P.M. so I can buy groceries etc. I expect that those sheets are lying in post office a long time, because I have not been to town since last Sat. I am glad to hear that you are willing to come up here. But will the children be contented and happy here and <u>no child will ever rule me</u>. I will be very strict that much I can say now. No cursing from anyone will be allowed. Mother is quite well according to Josephine's letter, and they may take a run to Whitewater soon. Those pictures are quite good. Just think what you have to show and only 7 years or eight older than I am. It would be all right if I had a few of my own here now to make it a real home. You wrote old sweetheart, do you want to rob a cradle. I'm only <u>thirty</u> past. Eight more years to make it thirty-eight. Ha Ha. I don't know when Mr. Werst is going to get his wife. I don't get to talk much with him lately. He is lucky to get one this fall anyway. I have to have patience with everything. Some people are more lucky than others. I'spose I would not have waited if I would have known this years ago. Maybe he will lose 100.00 pretty quick I can't afford to lose that much. If you never would have seen another soul except the children and me, how would you have seen the children? I don't know why tears come when you think of me. Maybe you wish that we never met, as you once told me. I got 1 qt. of milk since you left, but will have Schoenrock bring a qt. every day as long as he will work here. He wants to clear the rest of my land for $12.50 per Acre. That is cut the wood, brush, and pile the brush, but cut it better than what the Indians have done. But then Mr. Buhler will have to finance me for that much. Maybe I will get most of this land plowed this fall. Mr. Buhler said that we may not have the tractors next year. I'll try to get plowed as much as possible.

Sincerely yours, Ernst. H. W.

September 7, 1923, McGrath, Minnesota

Dear Myrtle,

Your letter of Tuesday evening was rec'd to-day, and I am sorry that I made you feel bad and sick. Please forgive me. I wrote you once or told you that I never wanted to make you feel bad again and now I have done it anyhow. I am not sick, but I do want you when you get ready to come. I have rec'd the eats today and it all is in very fine condition. Just as tho I would get it at your place. Thank you very much for it. My supper to-night was mostly from you. The bread which I had was a little mouldy and I just have one egg. I ate a quick supper because I felt as tho I ought to answer you as soon as possible and having a chance to ride to town to-nite with Mr. A Gunnufson I will then mail it. I don't care to have you spend so much to send eats, but they are appreciated more than ever. Mr. Paul Schoenrock had dinner with me and Gunnufson drove to the mailbox and brot the eats just as we were at eating dinner. Mr. Schoenrock told me to write you that the cake was very good, awful good, or in short d___ good. Don't bother to send me money because you need it as much as I do. I think that I will get some later and then you can use yours when you need it. I am glad that you can get so much coal at a time. Thank you for wanting to do my washing, but I can take time to do it and will not be very busy in a few weeks. I do hope that you can get a girl so you can take it easier too. I am glad to hear that you would like it up here. But wouldn't you like it better to be somewhere else if I were there. You know you can't get fresh meats and many other things here every day in the year. The thought has come to me that maybe you done that account of me and was keeping more boarders. Don't worry and work so hard for me now. I would sooner you take it more easy and let me do as much as I can. I do think of you very often just about all the spare time, not only when I eat the eats. I will work and live for you after this, let you plan our buildings etc. I wish that you could be up here when time comes to build the house and barns. The women ought to plan their house at all times and I do want you to have it your way, so you will be contented. Don't sell your good furniture. I don't think that it would cost much if you rented a car. You can't buy much up here to amount of anything. Yes I do believe you, and you have done more for me than I would ask from my folks. If I would have known that you borrowed so much then I could have saved on furniture. Please do not send any more until you have yours paid. I don't want you to have debt for my account. I had Mr. Gunnufson do blasting for me to-day. We have the big stumps from about 12 acres all blasted.

Expect to ride to town with him to-nite. I ate a quick supper and let the dishes unwashed, so I could write you before he would come. Thank you for the eats, and the washing. You surely have done up the shirt just lovely. It is a cool day here today. A regular fall day. Tomorrow the plasterers will finish here. Mr Schoenrock has gone after a load of white sand for me this P.M. You can call me Sweetheart if you like too. I know that you are mine. I will plan and surely expect to have you some day, and it can not be too soon. Good nite,

Sincerely yours, Ernst H.

P.S. Mr. Werst called on me for a few minutes before we rode to town here. He bought his furniture but did not have time to talk to him much. I have my sweater on and yet it was cold coming in town. It's 8:15 P.M. now.

September 11, 1923, McGrath, Minnesota

Dear Myrtle,

Your both letters have been rec'd yesterday and I am glad to get them too. Its Tuesday 11:15 A.M. and I am at cooking my dinner. Mr. Paul Schoenrock is helping his neighbor thresh to-day. It has been quite cold this morning, frost in the low meadow Mr. Crouch said. I stayed in bed until near 7 A.M. then after I had breakfast and the dishes done I walked to Crouch's and got a pail of water, also some cherry, and plum jelly which she gave me. Then I walked to Silver Star way to Vetelson's and made arrangement to have him or Mr. Henskie drive to Veteransville to-morrow P.M. I bought 400# Picric Acid but Mr. Henskie wants 100# so I will have 300# and I have 25 sticks of dynamite left. That will be enough explosives to clear the entire forty. All used and bought amounts to 523 lbs. Mr. Buhler offered it to me for $40.00 the whole 400#. We had paid $14.13 pr. hundred before. I got the three boxes 12.39 cheaper than when it has been sold here. Of course it will cost some to get it hauled, but I will be about $7.39 or more to the gain. I gave Mr. Buhler a note for that forty which can be paid at anytime. You see I am having debt now too, and he made me a promise to loan me sufficient money to get the entire forty cleared. But I still am in need of money. I owe the lumber yard $117.61 and then have to have enough to get the finishing work done in my house. I got some of my sweetcorn on the stove now, also some potatoes. Have three burners lit and everything is cooking now 11:35 A.M. The last few days are cooler. Is'pose you folks will have it in a few days too. So far the frost has not done much damage yet. I just turned off one burner now 11:39 A.M. I am thinking that you are busy at cooking too. Intend to clean up in the house, the plaster from the floor and maybe repile some lumber this P.M. You better save the shirts at your place because will not make use of them here this fall or winter. I have one silk shirt which I don't wear here now. It is different when a person has a woman who does the washing. Thank you very much for them tho. Tuesday P.M. 1:02 o'clock. I may just as well finish this while it is comfortable in this garage. It gets quite chilly nites and mornings. I ate about five little cobs of sweetcorn this noon, potatoes with butter, bread and jelly a roll and a cup full of hot water. That plum jelly is good which Mrs. Crouch gave me this morning. This may seem as a joke but it's true. I don't remember the day but anyhow one day last week I woke up quite early and have been quite much wake that morning. I'spose it will be a long time before you can have a talk with me. So you have thought of the brush and when we let the fires go out. We were hauling all P.M. yesterday such leavings of the brush piles, but still have that on the place where we had the talk to pick up yet. It will keep us busy for another day or more. Then I intend to have Mr. Schoenrock help me do the blasting which will take about a day or two. I am a bit tired of being alone, but I don't want you to rent your house to come up here. The children have it much better there than what they could have it here. Your children are much more to you than I am and I would not think much of you if you rented your house and came up here this fall. I have written just as the thoughts come to me and I will not deny it either. You know as well and better than I do that it is quite difficult to satisfy five, much more so than just one. A person who raises one after another gets more used to it than to get a houseful at once. The responsibility is what makes me stop to consider quite often. I will always be very stricked and will not allow profane language from no one. You see if Ralph is away from home 9 or 10 months of each year, and he is only a child. How do you suppose that you can tell him anything. The worst years are from 18–25 I believe. I don't care to have another man stay with me, because then I could not rest as well as now. Unless I knew that he was a neat gent and who would not care to run around much at nite. You don't write as you think, because you wrote maybe got some on that $100.00. Now you know we would never even tho you would want to. I will never marry for that reason, and don't think that I will try to win it. I don't think that I ought to talk to Buhler about your house. It would look as tho I am coaxing you up here, but you could write to him if you care to. All I heard about the state bonus that we were to get it after November 1. You never sent me the clippings about the soldiers pay. I don't know, but it would be fairly good if we could help each other some fine day. Maybe I'll help a day when I get to Wisconsin next year Ha. Ha. You don't mean just one day do you? Those ready cut houses cost much more because you have to add the labor to build them, which means quite much now days. The best is all a person can do, but you knew that before. I told you that I would not ask the folks for money, but I may ask them to borrow some for me and I will pay it and interest when payable if I can. We had rain Saturday A.M. and yesterday morning too. Will go to work and write more later 2:08 P.M. and quite nice out too.

Wed. Morning 7:25 A.M. Paul Schoenrock is working on the field and I told him that I wanted to write a bit yet so he said, send her my regards too. I cleaned the plaster mostly from the floor yesterday P.M. Had to knock it off with the hammer then scrape it with the hoe and shovel. Last nite Mr. Crouch asked me whether I wanted to ride to town, to see that show. I did but there was no show. It rained a little here last nite, and I think they did not care to show anyhow. I rec'd your letter and two from home yesterday. I got yours and one from home last nite. How late does Everett come in when he stays at your place. I'spose in the morning. I would not allow it. My ceiling in the house is low I can more than reach it from standing on the floor. Easy to swat flies, but I wish it was a ft. higher. It will do temporary and later it may be used for something else. Yes Ralph has done very well this summer. I have only been to church once since I am in this state. I am glad to hear that you are going to church, because that is what makes the children feel more as going when their parents go. If mother don't believe in going why should they. Thats what they may think otherwise. And it's true too. It's quite cold in this garage now. Good bye.

Sincerely yours, Ernst. K.

September 15, 1923, McGrath, Minnesota, 8:45 P.M.

Dear Myrtle,

Saturday nite and I just read your letter which I rec'd to-day. The one with the other in it. Mr. Werst brot it as far as the mail box this A.M. but I did not know it. To-nite when I walked to Crouch's for a pail of water then Werst came from town again with a load of furniture and asked me whether I got the box of eats and letter. I got it after 6 o'clock. The pears are all rotten and the box being soaked from the rotten pears broke open, but I think there was not much lost. I anyway got a loaf of bread 2 oranges, maybe one orange got lost it almost looked that way. The brown cake was all right but the nut and raisin cake was quite soaked and broken. I ate that for supper to-nite and also one piece of the brown cake which was soaked some. Thank you for the eats. Yesterday when we rode passed Gunnufson's with a load of sand, I run in and asked whether she had a loaf of bread to spare. She asked me what kind I wanted, Graham or wheat, and I said both. At first she did not want to sell two, but she wrapped up the both loafs and said I might as well let you have them. Today we got some more sand and I drove there cows which had broken out in the pasture again, then she said that I would get a qt. of milk for that. Mrs. Paul Schoenrock sent a whole pumpkin pie to me this morning. That graham bread was real fresh and I ate over a half a loaf last nite for supper (small loaves). Rode to town last nite with Mr. Gunnufson to buy groceries. The eats must have come this morning also the letter. Mother must be getting along fine now. How is she anyway?

I have the house all banked up with gravel sand, so the mice can't work in under. First I packed small stones between the others yet. I tacked tar paper around it and then banked the sand against it. Today we banked up around this garage. It is much warmer to-day. After 4 P.M. today I washed some underwear, socks, handkerchief. Walked to Crouch for water 3 times this P.M. and to the mail box. Last

Thursday and Friday, yesterday we had heavy frost. It surely was cold in this garage lately mornings and nites but is quite warm to-night. It is all banked up around it now which helps a great deal too. I think that I will not move in the house until after the 1st, because the plaster has to dry some more and Monday I will have 2 more men. The big tractor is supposed to be here Monday to pull stumps. Mr. Calhoun who has Washburn's job told me so and he also brot me a root hook so I can pull all the poplar stumps which are cut low and are too big to plow under. Mrs. Dougherty will board them for me. She expects to have some hunters soon but is willing to help me out. You surely don't have to take much from the boarders this year, now that there are so many. Is Irma tamed down any? She is a genuine I think, but you surely love her otherwise you would not have taken so much from her, and Ella. You are not as particular as I am, in such things. Yes Mrs. Gunnufson was along last Sunday. It is 9:40 P.M. and it has just started to rain now. It seemed to me as tho it would rain soon because I must so much to-day. I had a nice bath to-nite. No I have not spilled any for a long time. I don't have my mind on such so much now days. It don't do me any good so what is the use of thinking about it. The kind I would want I will not get, so I will never relish that, but it may not be half bad yet! That's one thing that is not the way I really like it, but if that will be the only thing, then it will not be so bad yet. I think that you are mistaken about that second mortgage. Your folks may have the second mortgage now. Another party may have a mortgage on the same farm and that party may have the 1st mortgage. Your folks may have the second altho it is the 1st papers. I think it is all right tho the way you have done it. I do not want to use any of your money. I want to make good with my own, and you need it as long as you have a cent of debt and I advise you to pay those first. Your silks will look more becoming to you when you have no debt. I have written to the folks to borrow some for me and I want to pay it back and the interest too, unless they want to give it to me that's up to them. The eats reminds me of something, what is left is good, but it is not all to be relished, the pears I can not relish anymore. They must have been too ripe when packed. Good nite will write more tomorrow. It's getting cool in here.

Sunday A.M. 10:40 I am all shaved, washed and dressed up—but—no way to go to church. Have been swatting flies. I don't like them around me anymore than people who powder. I have not slept well last nite I went to bed after 10:15 and another mouse must have gotten in here which I heard later. I got up and looked around but did not see it. Then after that, one of those (Millers) as you call them, was flying around the window so much that I got up again and killed that. Well at 3 o'clock I woke again and have not slept much since. At shortly after 6 o'clock some hunters were shooting around here. Hunting season is open now. I had an awful dream this morning. I dreamed that I was carrying a corpse. Just had a visitor Hansen was here for a short visit. Well I don't think that you care to read about my dream, it was not much, only as tho I was carrying Ed on a stretcher on the streets in Watertown. Two others where carrying at the head end. It does seem funny how a person does dream sometimes. I think it was because I was thinking of the farm and how we fooled around etc. as I was boarding at your place. It is nice out to-day. Quite warm but windy. I have 3/4 of that pumpkin pie to eat yet. I will not make very much for dinner. I have fruit lemons and bread, cake, cookies. Will have a few wieners tho. Sunday P.M. 1:05 it is quite windy out here but nice and warm. I am thinking that you are having company from Watertown to-day. I ate 1/4 of that pie yesterday and another piece this noon. I found a part of a fly in it and that spoiled it all now. I will write to the folks and Sis. Amanda yet. Good bye,

Sincerely yours, Ernst H.

P.S. Gunnufson's horses were here last Sunday and are here again to-day. Some callers Ha ha. Do what seems best to you with the money because I will not use your money. I still owe you some the way it is, which will be paid back soon. That letter is written with pencil and would not be any good to you at all in court. I do hope that you get it tho, then you will have nothing to worry about.

# Bibliography


Anderson, G. W. *Atlas of Buffalo County, Nebraska.* Mason City, Iowa. Nebraska: Anderson Publishing Company, 1919.

Barton, Ruth Ann. *The Schools of Our Past: Typical Pioneer Schools.* Palmyra, Wisconsin: Palmyra Historical Society, 1989.

Cook, Philip L. *Zion City Illinois: 20th Century Utopia.* Syracuse, New York: Syracuse University Press, 1996.

*Crimes and Punishment: The Illustrated Crime Encyclopedia.* Westport, Connecticut: H. S. Stuttman Co., 1994.

Derleth, August. *Wisconsin Murders.* Sauk City, Wisconsin: Mycroft and Moran, 1968.

Gnacinski, Janneyne Longley. *Sullivan, Town 6 North: A History of the Town of Sullivan, Jefferson County, Wisconsin.* Waukesha, Wisconsin: Freeman Printing Company, 1970.

Newton, Michael. *Bad Girls Do It: An Encyclopedia of Female Murderers.* Port Townsend, Washington: Loompanics Unlimited, 1993.

Pierce, Clara Howell. *Historical Gleanings of Melendy's Prairie.* Palmyra, Wisconsin: Palmyra Historical Society, 1970.

Sents, Aeilt E. *The Methodist Episcopal Church* (pamphlet). Whitewater, Wisconsin: 1997.

Whitewater Historical Society. *125th Anniversary: 1837–1962: Whitewater June 30–July 1-2-3-4.* Whitewater, Wisconsin: Whitewater Historical Society, 1962.

Whitewater State Normal School. *1921 Minneiska.* Whitewater, Wisconsin: 1921.

# Index

# E



# F



# G



# H



# I



# J



# L



# M

## W



## Y



## Z